© Kleinpeter Photography

About the Author

JEFF D. OPDYKE is a financial columnist and the author of six books, including most recently *Financially Ever After* and *Piggybanking*. During Opdyke's seventeen years at *The Wall Street Journal*, he wrote about personal finance, family finance, and the investment markets, and for six of those years he wrote the popular and nationally syndicated Love & Money column. He lives in Baton Rouge, Louisiana, with his wife, Amy, and their two children.

Protecting Your Parents' Money

Also by Jeff D. Opdyke

*Piggybanking: Preparing Your Financial Life
for Kids and Your Kids for a Financial Life*

*Financially Ever After: The Couples'
Guide to Managing Money*

Love & Money: A Life Guide to Financial Success

*The Wall Street Journal
Complete Personal Finance Guidebook*

*The Wall Street Journal Personal
Finance Workbook*

*The World Is Your Oyster: The Guide to
Finding Great Investments Around the Globe*

Protecting Your Parents' Money

The Essential Guide to
Helping Mom and Dad Navigate
the Finances of Retirement

Jeff D. Opdyke

HARPER
BUSINESS

HARPER

BUSINESS

The Wall Street Journal® is a registered trademark of Dow Jones and is used by permission of Dow Jones.

HarperCollins books may be purchased for educational, business, or sales promotional use. For information please write: Special Markets Department, HarperCollins Publishers, 10 East 53rd Street, New York, NY 10022.

FIRST EDITION

Designed by John Lewis

Bird nest illustration on page v © Suzanne Clements/iStockphoto

Library of Congress Cataloging-in-Publication Data is available upon request.

ISBN 978-0-06-135820-3

11 12 13 14 15 OV/RRD 10 9 8 7 6 5 4 3 2

To Amy, Zachary, and Nicole
for putting up with yet *another* of my book projects.
I love you.

Contents

Introduction

THERE IS A REASON you picked up this book. Likely it's because you're over the age of thirty-five and you are facing a situation few adult children want to face, much less know how to deal with: having to parent your parents financially because they've reached or are quickly reaching an age—either physically or mentally—where they can no longer do so themselves.

Some of you are scrambling for answers now, having been thrown into this situation unexpectedly. Others are feeling less pressured, though no less concerned, because while you're not yet enveloped in the tempest you nevertheless see exactly what's coming. You want the answers to your questions before the issues arrive.

Whatever your particular situation, you've found the right book. In these pages you will learn what you need to know to help Mom or Dad or both navigate the finances of aging—from understanding nursing homes and how to pay for them to the pros and cons of annuities and structuring a stream of income to live on in retirement, and from understanding what Medicare and Medicaid do and don't cover to collecting Social Security benefits and calculating whether or when a reverse mortgage makes sense as a financial option.

But before we begin with all that, know this: You are not alone. In fact, you're part of quite a large crowd of people, all across the country, struggling with many of the very same issues and questions swirling around your head. Roughly a quarter of all U.S. households are providing some form of care to a relative over the age of fifty, according to the National Alliance for Caregiving. A USA Today/ABC News/ Gallup poll found that 41% of baby boomers with a living parent were caring for that parent in some fashion. Numerous other polls and surveys found much the same results.

Whatever the actual number, some of the care being provided clearly falls into the broad category of personal and/ or family finance—be it paying Mom's bills or helping Dad shop for a long-term care policy.

Chances are you don't know everything you need to know to effectively guide a parent through the decisions that need to be made.

Indeed, for millions of people dealing with an aging parent, the answers don't come easily. Many of the underlying topics are complicated and so heavily nuanced that there can be no one-size-fits-all solution, or even a one-size-fits-many solution. Often each answer is as unique as each family.

To that end, this book doesn't set out to provide you with a personalized, turn-by-turn guide for each challenge you're likely to face with aging parents. Too many permutations exist to make that feasible.

Instead, this book offers a broad road map for navigating

the issues that arise. Some of the advice you'll find in these pages you can easily take on yourself. But a big part of parenting your parents is knowing not only what you do know, but knowing what you don't—and how to find the experts you need or how to tap into the various resources that exist to help you help Mom/Dad.

Either way, the information in this book aims to make you a better advocate for and protector of your parents. To put you in the right frame of mind: Think back on how you felt as a young kid, when your parents had all the answers (or at least seemed to). That's the role you're called to play when you step in to parent your parents through the last phase of life. You are now the one with all the answers.

Thus, my job in this book is to help you:

- understand what you need to know about the topics that are germane to parenting your parents, and where it's appropriate I will explain some of the tricks you need to be aware of in order to make helping your parents easier on you;
- locate the assistance and services you need in whatever state your parent lives in; and
- provide tips along the way for more easily and more effectively parenting your parents financially.

Throughout the book, I've included "Conversation Starters" that you can use verbatim to start these tough, sometimes painful conversations with your parents. If you don't like my language, or if it sounds wrong for your parents, no worries, tweak it however you see fit. It's in here just to give you a general sense of what you need to say and how.

You'll also find a lot of terms in this book that I've placed in bold type. These are the words you'll find in the "Terms to Know" section of the appendix, in case you're not familiar with the word or the concept it defines. If you don't need this refresher, great, you're already ahead of the game. However, I understand that not everyone has had the best personal finance education. And that's OK, too. The important fact is that you're stepping in to help your parents, and to make that as easy as possible. I'm including the "Terms to Know" section as a quick reference to help you.

So it's time to finally address those worries you have inside. The first step in the process starts on the next page—learning to communicate with Mom/Dad. It's the most important step in the process you're about to begin.

1

The Talk

THIS IS THE SINGLE most important chapter in this book. I placed it first in line for one overarching reason: Just about everything else you will read in these pages—and all your efforts at helping Mom and Dad manage or deal with the financial aspects of aging—will work out so much easier for you and your family if you first learn to communicate with your parents.

Everybody thinks they know how to communicate because, well, we've all spent thirty or forty or fifty years or more expressing our thoughts and feelings and emotions. We've learned how to talk to one another. So, really, how difficult can chatting with parents be? Just ask the questions for which you want answers and then catalog what Mom and Dad say.

Good luck with that.

I promise that for many, many families the necessary answers won't be that easy to pry loose. Just as you are likely quite private with your own finances, your parents are just as private with theirs. They easily could look suspiciously on your unexpected queries about their money, what they spend their Social Security checks on, where their bank accounts are located, and their plans for distributing an estate when they pass on. As such, don't be surprised when Mom or Dad or both delicately or brusquely brush aside your advances, stall providing adequate answers, or even express outright worry or anger over perceptions that you might be out to wrest control of their financial freedom or, worse, rob them of their assets before they're dead. Dramatic? Yes. However, the news in the last decade or so has been filled with so many sad tales of elderly victims of financial abuse, statistically perpetrated most often by a family member, that aging parents at times can't help but question a child's intentions. In short, Mom and Dad, at least in their own minds, have real reason to fear your unwanted intrusion into their personal financial lives. As a result, the answers you want aren't always as forthcoming as you might expect.

And those parents who do want to talk, meanwhile, the ones who implicitly trust their children and want their kids involved in making the big and small decisions of old age, don't always know how to tell you what they want to say for fear that you don't want to hear it. They don't know how to ask the questions that have them concerned, and they worry they'll be thought of as stupid or financially incompetent. Sometimes they simply don't know how to begin the conversation.

Parents, of course, aren't the only ones incapable of expressing themselves. Kids, too, feel intimidated asking Mom and Dad highly personal questions about an aspect of their lives that might always have been private. Kids often assume parents don't want to talk, and so they never raise the questions they need answers to in order to understand whether their parents might need help with some part of the day-to-day finances. Others simply refuse to contemplate Mom or Dad's mortality.

This lack of communication can be a major problem in the unique relationship between elderly parents and their grown children. Because once it's too late, it's much too late. When a parent falls ill or dies, you're suddenly thrown into the tempest—unprepared for all you will have to confront in managing the situation. Take, for example, the simple safe-deposit box. All you need to know is the location of the bank and the key to get into it, right? And since you already know where Mom banks and the desk drawer where she keeps the key, you've got that covered; you know that when the moment comes you can at least access the box to gather the paperwork she's kept stuffed in there ever since you were a kid.

However, you're in for a stressful confrontation with that bank at precisely the moment in life when additional stress is the last burden you want. When you try to access the safe-deposit box, Mom's banker will bar you, legally, from even entering the vault if you're not listed on the account. While some states will allow heirs or executors to access a safe-deposit box when an owner dies, that's not the case everywhere. So when you're in desperate need of the will or the insurance contract or burial papers or some other document you know is in that box, you might find you have no access. You'll have to hire a lawyer to help you jump through the various hoops required to prove that you legally have a right to open the box. Had you and your parents had the appropriate discussion about what's in the safe-deposit box and how they want to handle who has access to it in an emergency, you wouldn't be in such a frustrating position when emotions are already running high and the last complication you want is an inability to provide for your parents.

It all begins with a few simple words: "Mom, Dad . . . can we talk?"

When to Have The Talk

LIFE IS RARELY CONSIDERATE enough to dish up a perfect moment for every key episode we must live through. In some families an event might transpire that clearly exclaims in its subtext, "Now is that perfect moment. Act!" That could be the death of one parent, a hospitalization that leaves Mom or Dad incapable of handling money matters, or it could be a financial emergency in which a parent seeks money from you to cover an expense. If those situations arise in your life, take advantage of them in the moment and have The Talk.

Not every family will have that opportunity, though, and the absence of a dramatic event doesn't negate the need to talk to parents about their finances. Instead you'll have to fabricate a perfect moment, and, well, there's no time like the present—because you just never know what the future might hold or how soon that future might arrive.

The time to initiate The Talk is when questions about your parents' financial self-sufficiency become an issue you spend time thinking about yourself. Unless your only concern is when you're going to get your hands on your parents' money (and that's not a healthy concern), thoughts about their financial life generally don't just pop into your head without reason. You've probably noticed something subconsciously—maybe even overtly—when you're with your parents or when you're talking to them. Pay attention to those instincts. You might not immediately be able to pinpoint exactly what has you concerned, and that's fine. The point isn't to immediately recognize the worrisome issue, but rather that you are worried and that you want to better understand your parents' finances so that you can assist them effectively, if and when the times comes to do so.

Sometimes parents will signal when they want to have The Talk. So listen to what they say and pay attention to the context. A parent, for instance, might be fretting about paper losses suffered in the stock market or worrying about replacing a car, and they're seeking your advice. Maybe they're complaining about a large medical bill or an overdue utility statement that has destroyed their budget. Such comments might well be a parent's way of trying to draw you into a conversation they've wanted to have with you for a while but were afraid to initiate for any number of reasons. Pounce on those opportunities. This is your chance to open up a much more thorough discussion about their finances without having to be the one to broach the subject first.

Whatever the case, remember that you're not just helping your parents; you're helping yourself and your own family. Ultimately, helping your parents manage their finances means you're running two households—yours and theirs—and anything you can do now to prepare for that possibility will be preparation well worth the effort.

So initiate The Talk sooner rather than later.

Breaking the Ice

MONEY IS TABOO, no two ways about it. More times than not, people are reluctant to share the innermost details of their wallet, even with their own offspring, out of fear they'll soon be separated from their own money in some reprehensible fashion.

That taboo is particularly strong among the elderly, who typically grew up in an era where money simply wasn't discussed openly among family members. Think back: Did your parents talk to you about their income, household expenses, or budgeting worries? Probably not. And that probably hasn't changed all these years later.

Along with privacy, there's also the issue of pride. Every adult wants to feel capable of managing the finances of daily living. Indeed, starting at an early age money management is a large part of what many of us define as independence. Even when young kids first begin to learn that green paper can be traded for toys at the store, they want to be able to control their own (albeit limited) financial resources—if only to buy as many toys as they can. Little wonder, then, that broaching the subject of Mom or Dad's personal finances naturally raises defenses in parents who have been in control of their own pocketbook for decades. And some people, even in their dotage, simply do not want to be reminded of their mortality, which is clearly a central point when you ask your parents about the end-of-life issues that are inherent in The Talk.

As such, breaking the ice is a game of perception. If you come on too forcefully, as though you are trying to commandeer their money for their own good, Mom and Dad will shut down, concerned that you might only be after their money for your own uses. If you come off too meekly, as though you're just a friend asking if everything is OK, they'll easily deflect your questions and say, "We're fine; there's no reason to worry about us, Honey," or something along those lines.

You want an approach somewhere in the middle of that spectrum. On one hand, you want to be heartfelt and sincere. On the other, you should be clear that while you might not try to delve into every last aspect of their financial life, you're not taking no for an answer because understanding how you might be called on to help or take control of assets and bills and whatnot in an emergency is that important to you.

Some personal finance publications encourage a backdoor approach to this conversation and suggest you start by sharing your own experiences first—something like: "You know my retirement plan really took a beating in the market crash. How is your account holding up?" Some suggest using the "I have a friend" approach, as in: "I have a friend and this, that, and the other thing just happened to his/her mom/dad. Has anything like that happened to you?"

I'm not saying don't try these approaches; they might work with some parents. But they are tepid at best and easily brushed aside by parents who feel uncomfortable talking to you about such a personal subject, regardless of your own experiences or those of that "friend."

The best approach is at once the simplest and, for some people, the most difficult:

"Mom/Dad, I want to talk to you about your money. I know it's a private matter, and I know you might not feel entirely comfortable talking about it at this very moment, but I'd like to make some time to sit down with you and understand your finances so that if anything ever happens I can help you deal with it in whatever way you need me to help. If there are financial items or accounts that you don't want me to know about, that's fine. But I would like to know what accounts and what documents are necessary for managing your household, your health, or your finances in an emergency or when you pass away."

Direct. Honest.

True, summoning the gumption to raise the issue might not be as easy as that simple string of words might suppose. And your parents might not immediately open their wallet to reveal the secrets to their financial kingdom right then and there. But they're much more likely to respect your approach because it clearly leaves them in control of the process and tells them you're not out for selfish gains. Moreover, they are quite likely to see that you're being sincere about wanting to be there to help them when they ultimately need the help of someone they want to be able to trust. That will go a long way in setting a parent's mind at ease. And even if your parents aren't inclined to open up at the moment you raise the topic, there's a very good chance you will receive a phone call in the not-too-distant future with an offer to sit down and talk about finances. When that day arrives, you're also quite likely to find that Mom/Dad is not only willing to talk, they might even have an envelope waiting for you that contains the keys to their personal financial vault: the locations of their accounts, copies of their insurance policies and other important paperwork, and instructions on how they want you to handle their end-of-life issues.

For parents who do want to talk but have been just as anxious as you about diving headlong into such a potentially emotionally charged conversation, breaking the ice in a direct, honest manner gives them the entry they've been looking for. They might jump at the chance to finally open up and share with you all this information they've been waiting to divulge. At the end of the day, the elderly want to feel secure, and part of that security comes in knowing there is someone they can trust with their finances.

Some people, of course, will still feel queasy questioning Mom or Dad directly about money and end-of-life preparations. If the spoken word is a problem for you, then write a letter or e-mail. Your note—again, honest and direct—should clearly explain what you're seeking. Detail why the information is so important to you—and stress that you want to be able to help effectively when that help is needed most. Also explain honestly why you're writing a letter instead of talking face-to-face (maybe you feel uncomfortable talking about this issue with the people you love most because it raises in your own mind those issues of Mom and Dad's mortality; maybe you know you'll get too emotional talking to them directly; maybe you're trying to provide your parents a level of privacy that a personal meeting doesn't necessary allow; or maybe you're worried a face-to-face chat would come off as too intimidating to your parents, so you're taking another tack that provides for an easier discourse).

If in a face-to-face meeting your parents are clearly uncomfortable with your questions, offer them the same option of dealing with this in a letter or e-mail. That can be substantially easier on their sensibilities, since it gives them the opportunity over days or weeks to think about what they really want you to know, to consider the benefits of having someone they can trust look out for their best interests, and to gather the data they want to share. After that you can go back, if necessary, and ask questions that will help fill in whatever holes might still exist in your knowledge about your parents' finances.

None of this means, of course, that your parents have to play ball. For whatever reason, they can still say no to your advances, and there's nothing you can do about it. Unless Mom/Dad clearly shows signs of a medical issue that prevents them from acting in their own best interest, you cannot force yourself on their pocketbook. You can ask. You can try to be persuasive. You can provide ample evidence that you want to protect and help them and that you will stay clear of their accounts until you're asked to step in. But if the answer is no, well, then the answer is no and your only choice is to back off—graciously. You've made your concerns known and if your parents ever reach a point where they want help—or need help—they know they can turn to you.

What *Not* to Say

IT'S A STAPLE OF weeknight sitcoms: the inappropriate comment that suddenly quashes the protagonists' efforts up to that point. The same problem arises all the time, as well, when otherwise well-meaning adult children endeavor to help their parents. You say the wrong thing or take the wrong tone, or your parents simply perceive your words and tone the wrong way, and suddenly your efforts are dead in the water. As such, what you *don't* say—and how you say what you *do* say—are crucial factors in The Talk.

Thus, the primary rule: Avoid *anything* that sounds like blame. Criticism and condescension are off the list, too. Never utter statements such as: "You brought this on yourself." "This is all your fault." "If you had listened to me instead of _____ " "You don't understand" (which implies your parent isn't as smart as you). "You really screwed this up."

Think about yourself. How do you typically respond when people criticize you, condescend to you, belittle your actions, or try to make you feel rotten because decisions you've made have, after the fact, proven less than stellar? You're angry, yes. But you're probably mad at yourself already, so the last poke you want is from family or friends who make you feel worse. More to the point, in these instances you're not terribly inclined to listen to whatever prescriptive advice that critic is offering. Instead, you're more likely to write off this person as, essentially, a jerk.

Parents are no different. The worst action you can take is to get mad, raise your voice, yell, or threaten to take control of your parent's finances anyway or to seek legal advice in helping you take control. Such outbursts and threats only highlight parental worries that your true interests lie with the money—not Mom/Dad's well-being.

Along these same lines, do not impose your will or take control of situations, accounts, or decisions until a parent asks you to do so. (Clearly, in an emergency, if Mom or Dad falls ill or is somehow incapable of managing his or her financial life, you must impose your will out of necessity, but that's a very different circumstance than the requirements of daily personal finance.) A parent might ultimately want you in charge, but it's a decision you want your mom or dad to come to and voice independently. Parents aren't always looking to you to assume control of their finances; in many instances, they simply want your input because they value it or because they trust that you will lead them in the appropriate direction even as they maintain financial autonomy over their own wallet.

As such, when talking to parents about their money, their financial decisions, bequeaths they expect to make, and other end-of-life issues, structure your comments and questions to emphasize the word *you*, as in: "So, how do *you* want to handle this?" or "What can I do to help *you* manage this issue?" With this approach you're empowering your parents and deemphasizing whatever self-interests you might have, allowing your parents to focus instead on the needs they want to address.

There's another reason for this approach: Some parents will already know the solution they want to pursue and bringing you into the equation is a way of bouncing their ideas off someone they trust. Or they may do so because they need your help in some fashion to execute their plan. Other parents won't have a clue about what they want to do or how they want you to help, generally because they're not even sure what their options are or how to determine the options that exist. Under those circumstances they'll turn back on you the very question you asked of them: "How do you want to manage this?" Once again, you don't want to offer solutions that seem to put you in charge of their money or somehow appear to lock them out of the ultimate decision-making process. Instead, you can approach this a couple ways; for example, you can:

- offer to research the issue and then report back with multiple options that you two can then discuss together to determine which path your parent thinks best fits the need;
- suggest that you both visit with a family law attorney, a financial planner, an estate planner, or whatever expert is most appropriate to the situation; this way you are obtaining with your parent unbiased, independent advice—and that independence will help buffer you against any complaints that might arise from a parent or siblings (and those complaints arise within families far too often to be overlooked).

Certainly, if you have specific expertise, like, say, in law or investing, then offering up your ideas is fine, so long as your ideas clearly benefit your parent and wouldn't be seen by a third-party observer as somehow benefiting you. You must act as though you are your parents' personal **fiduciary**, and that means every action you take on your parents' behalf must be unmistakably in their best interest, even if those actions ultimately mean you lose out on some or even all of your inheritance.

I know some people who will scoff at that, specifically grown-ups who think Mom and Dad are effectively babysitting the nest egg they built over all those years simply for their children to collect one day. If you share that mentality, you might consider begging off of any request for assistance your parent makes, because you risk making decisions that will cause untold friction, ill will, and fights that have cleaved many a family. Tread exceedingly carefully in that world.

Topics for The Talk

BEFORE YOU SET A time to talk to your parents—or before you sit down to write a letter or e-mail—you need to define what it is you want to know so that you can know what to ask.

The various subjects make up the rest of this book, but let's take a few minutes to broadly go over the information and data you need to know. You're looking to build as complete a picture of your parents' financial life as possible, because the more you know the easier for you when the time comes to step up and take over for your parents or to manage the various end-of-life duties you'll have to deal with.

Now, before we dive into the topics, I want you to know that in the appendix you'll find a worksheet—cleverly named "The Talk Worksheet." It catalogs in one place all the topics for The Talk, as well as the information you'll need to gather as part of the next chapter, "The Documents." The worksheet gives you a readymade agenda for the talk you have with Mom/Dad. All you need to do is fill out the worksheet as you're having the talk, and photocopy various documents. Then just keep the worksheet and the collection of papers together, and you're good to go; you'll have everything you need in one place so that you can quickly and efficiently deal with whatever issue arises.

Social Security Numbers, Birth Dates, Maiden Names, Middle Names, Previous Addresses, and Former Employers: The first two are crucial; the latter four can be quite useful. You will inevitably need to know Social Security numbers and birth dates to help your parents manage the various aspects of aging. Banks, investment firms, insurers, government agencies— just about any entity you can think of—will ask for this information so that the representative can track down the information you're seeking. So always have these handy when handling Mom/Dad's personal affairs. In nearly every case, of course, your parent must provide the company or agency permission—either verbally or in writing—to talk with you, or you will first need to send a notarized power of attorney that shows you legally can act on behalf of your parents.

Additionally, middle names, maiden names, previous addresses, and former employers can all be helpful in establishing identity or even tracking down long-forgotten retirement benefits.

Bank Accounts: Where do Mom and Dad do their banking? This is crucial information for obvious reasons: You have to know where their money is in order to make deposits or access their savings and checking to pay bills. Don't assume your parents operate from just one bank. Many people own multiple types of bank accounts, including money market accounts and certificates of deposit that they spread among multiple banks for any number of reasons, ranging from perceived safety to higher yields. So you'll need to ask your parents specifically if they have banking relationships aside from their primary bank, including online accounts.

Nor should you assume your parents will accurately recall every account. Elderly parents in particular might not remember all the accounts they own, especially CDs, which at maturity passively roll over from one period to the next, making it exceedingly easy after several years to forget a certain CD exists. That's particularly true if parents move from one state to another in retirement. They might purposefully leave behind a bank account in their previous city for when they visit friends and family or because the CD hasn't yet matured and they see no reason to move it—and then through the years that account slips the mind. Indeed, people often forget a variety of accounts exist when they don't routinely interact with them. For that reason, ask Mom and Dad if you can examine their files, looking for forgotten accounts. If they're hesitant, or if they balk at the thought of you rummaging through their personal documents, ask them to do so for you instead, explaining that you're simply trying to ensure that all of their assets are accounted for, for their own benefit.

TIP: Forgotten and lost accounts are commonplace. But there is a way to help locate those that might exist: Contact the governmental agency that catalogs unclaimed property in the state where your parents live, or have lived previously. These are often long-dormant bank accounts or accounts at other institutions that after a number of years revert to state control. Through that agency you can track down whatever unclaimed property might exist in a parent's name.

In most instances the appropriate agency is the state treasurer's office, though in some states a different agency might be in charge (still, the treasurer's office will be able to point you in the right direction). Check online as well. Many states post listings of residents for whom the state is holding unclaimed property. You'll have to prove who you are and that your parent is the rightful owner, but that's generally not terribly difficult.

Investment Accounts: These include brokerage accounts and individual retirement accounts (IRAs) at a brokerage firm, a bank or a mutual fund company, or 401(k) accounts with former employers. Monthly or quarterly account statements will exist somewhere, or you will see the name of a firm noted in your parent's annual income tax return. (And tax returns in general can be a good source of information on accounts that do exist, because any level of income generates some sort of tax form. You might have to contact Mom/Dad's accountant, with your parent's permission, to see past tax returns.)

Again, check with the state treasurer for unclaimed property. Brokerage firms and banks routinely end up as part of a competitor through an acquisition. Through the decades other competitors nab those original acquirers, leading to an all-too-common situation in which the financial firm where your parents originally opened an account is effectively lost after half a dozen acquisitions or more. If an acquiring firm can't find the owner of an old account it comes to own through the purchase of another bank or brokerage firm, that account ends up in the hands of those state agencies.

Pension Funds and Company-Sponsored Life and Health Insurance Policies: Many of today's aging parents have pensions paid by a former employer, though pensions are increasingly less common as companies do away with them to save costs.

Some also are covered by a company-sponsored group life insurance policy. As such, you'll need any employment information your parent might have so that you can jump in as necessary to handle a payment snafu that might emerge, or to claim the life insurance benefits when that time comes.

Also, work with Mom or Dad to rebuild their employment history as best they can remember. You or they might realize other forgotten retirement benefits exist. Some parents will have spent a career job hopping and, as with financial accounts, might have forgotten about benefits owed by a former employer. If Mom and Dad moved around as they job-hopped, an employer from earlier in their life could easily lose track of a former employee's whereabouts and have no idea where to send pension payments or how to provide other retiree benefits (see "Finding a Lost Pension" on page 106 to learn more).

As with financial firms, mergers in corporate America mean retiree benefits often switch from one company to another—and then to another and then another—making it increasingly difficult to backtrack and determine what happened to the pension or insurance to which your parent might be entitled. You'll find help, though, at the Pension Benefits Guaranty Corporation (PBGC), a government agency in Washington, DC, that takes over failed, troubled, or discontinued pension plans. (See the end of chapter 3, "The Money," for more information on the PBGC and tracking down potentially forgotten pensions.)

Safe-Deposit Boxes: Unless Mom and Dad have a safe in their house, chances are quite good they have a safe-deposit box at a local bank to hold all that they consider precious and important. And even if they do own a safe, they might still have a safe-deposit box.

Obviously you want to know about this box and what's in it. Some parents will recall everything in the box; others will remember a few things but forget others. To build a complete list, pay a visit to the bank with a parent to catalog the contents. You'll likely find precious metals like gold or silver (either bullion or, more commonly, coins), stock certificates, corporate or government bonds, savings bonds, cash, diamonds or other family heirloom jewelry, insurance policies, long-term care contracts, wills, trusts, burial documents, titles to cars, deeds to the house, and so on.

Perhaps most important when talking about the safe-deposit box is discussing the need to have your name on the bank's list of people who have access to that particular box. As noted earlier in this chapter, in some states if you're not on that list, you're not going to be able to gain access without a lawyer's assistance, even in an emergency. A friendly bank manager might, in an emergency, let you see a particular document in the safe-deposit box that you need to carry out some specific end-of-life wish—though that is not guaranteed. It's better, instead, to make sure your parents request that you be included as a renter or owner on the safe-deposit box or as someone who otherwise has access.

Finally, and rather obviously, you need to know where Mom and Dad keep the key to the safe-deposit box, since you'll need that to gain access. You don't want to find yourself scrounging through your parents' drawers, cabinets, and files hunting for a key at a moment when you need it quickly. The same logic applies if your parents, instead, keep their valuables and important papers in a home safe. Catalog the contents and make sure you know the combination to the lock and that you have the key, or at least know where your parents keep it hidden.

Insurance: As parents age, various forms of insurance become particularly important, and you're going to need to know the details of each policy so that when necessary you can effectively help manage health care and prescription drug plans, hospitalization coverage, Medicare/Medicaid benefits, long-term care benefits, and, ultimately, claim the death benefits of a life insurance contract.

Collect the contracts and make copies of the first pages that spell out the coverage, making sure you include policy numbers, the name of the insurance carrier, and the insurer's contact information. Keep those copies in a lockbox at home, rather than a bank's safe-deposit box, so that you can easily reference them when needed.

Wills, Trusts, and Other Estate Documents: You don't necessarily need to know what these documents state, and don't press for the details if parents seem reticent to share; for many people, how they plan to divide their estate (no matter how big or small) is a private matter that they want only their lawyers to know about until the appropriate time comes.

All you really need to know is where to find copies of the relevant documents so that you can access them at the appropriate moment. While parents will generally have copies of their wills and trusts either at home or in the safe-deposit box, in many cases your parents' lawyer will have copies of all the latest documents, so you might need to know only the lawyer's contact information. But beware: Always ask your parents where they keep their own copies, because in some situations the lawyer who prepared documents years ago might have retired and might either have not passed his clients to another attorney, or the acquiring law firm might have lost such old documents in the handover. Best to know where some version of the documents exists.

Burial Insurance and Funeral Instructions: Though relatively rare in comparison to other forms of insurance, burial insurance or prepaid funeral plans do pop up among the elderly who often want to make sure their death doesn't burden family members, or those who want to pick out the details of their burial or cremation.

At the most basic level you need to know where the policy is kept, the name of the funeral home where your parent has made arrangements, and any other germane requests Mom and Dad might have. Again, you might want a copy of the first few pages of this contract, and you should keep it at home in your own files, because if the end comes on a weekend, you might not have access to that bank safe-deposit box.

A Final Thought

REMEMBER, EVERYTHING IN THIS chapter is built on one key principle: respect. Recognizing that is paramount. Whether your parents approach you first or whether you initially approach them, you are engaging in one of the most intimate relationships possible: control over another person's financial well-being.

That intimacy is all the more poignant when your parents are the people you're caring for. The decisions you make on their behalf have direct and profound consequences on their health, their wealth, and their state of mind.

2

The Documents

IN SOME SAD WAY it's true: All of us are little more than a number somewhere in a system. By that I mean we go through life accumulating various accounts and, in so doing, accumulating a string of digits attached to our names so that some insurance company, some broker, some bank, mortgage company, health care provider, power generator—or whatever—can identify who we are, where we live, and what we own or owe. As the overseer of a parent's life, it will be your task to gather up and catalog all these scraps of identification and the underlying services, promises, assets, and liabilities they represent so that you can better manage Mom or Dad's affairs when one or both of them ask you to, or when they are unable to do so themselves.

The documents we're talking about fall into two broad categories: daily documents and long-range documents.

Daily documents are those that track the monthly or quarterly bills and statements: bank and brokerage statements, electricity and cable bills, pension/Social Security/**annuity** payments, premium-due notices that arrive from insurance firms, and others. These documents help you build a portrait of your parent's routine expenses and assets and liabilities, and will be exceedingly helpful when working with Mom/ Dad to construct a budget, which we'll get to in the next chapter, "The Money."

The long-range documents, meanwhile, are those that will come into play when you step in to help manage or take control of a parent's health care or finances, or when a parent passes away. Many of these are planning documents, such as a **will** or a **power of attorney**, though this category also includes items such as a mortgage or the title to a car that you will need at some point as well.

As you collect all this paperwork, you will need a filing system of some sort to keep all the papers straight and easily accessible. Use whatever method fits your personality or style—individual manila folders, an expandable accordion-type file folder with the individual letters of the alphabet printed on tabs so that you can file the electricity bills under *E*. Whatever you choose, just keep it as neat as possible; when an emergency does arise, you really don't want to have to rummage through a pile of papers you tossed into a box just to find the single account number and contact information you need to address the problem.

And a gigantic caveat: Always check with an attorney who lives in your parent's state and who specializes in **eldercare** and **estate planning** issues. The information in this chapter is as of 2010 and is largely generic, designed to give you a sense of what particular documents are important, but nothing in here should be construed as legal advice specific to you or your parents, since every family's needs are different and each state has its own sets of rules and laws that must be followed for any legal document to be considered valid.

Daily Documents

SINCE DAILY DOCUMENTS ARE the ones you will deal with most often, we'll start with them, and we'll start with the most important daily documents first: income and assets documents, since keeping track of the money coming in, and how much is available in savings and investment accounts, is so crucial in retirement. (Note: For each of the sections below, the bulleted items represent the information you need to know or catalog.)

Social Security/Pension/Annuity Checks

- *How much money does your parent receive each month from Social Security, a company pension, or any annuities that might exist?* You also want to know if the income is scheduled to increase on a regular basis. Social Security checks generally increase each year, tied to a cost-of-living adjustment, a so-called COLA. You can contact the annuity or pension provider to ask whether that income stream benefits from a COLA as well. This knowledge will help you with budgeting in the next chapter, "The Money."
- *Who are the payers and what is their contact information?* Clearly the government is sending the Social Security checks, but which insurance company is responsible for

the annuity payment, and which company is sending the monthly pension? The contact information you need includes phone number and address. Jot down a website address as well as any e-mail address that might be listed on the statement; they can come in handy.

• *What are the account numbers?* This is crucial information in the event you need to reach out to the payer. Obviously Mom/Dad's Social Security number is the identification number for the Social Security checks. An annuity will have a policy number, while a corporate pension will either be tied to the Social Security number or, possibly, an employee number.

• *How is this money handled?* Are the checks directly deposited into a bank account, or does Mom/Dad receive the physical check and then head to the bank to deposit the money? If the physical check is arriving each month, do yourself a favor and encourage your parent to sign up for **direct deposit** (or do it yourself for them, if you have power of attorney). The Social Security Administration offers that service, as do most insurers and company pension plans. With direct deposit you won't have to worry about whether your parent remembered to make the deposit, nor will you have to worry about the check getting lost in the mail or at home. It also negates any possibility that a housekeeper, home health aide, or some other person with access to your Mom/Dad can doctor a check or somehow convince your parent to sign it over. Some retirees are squeamish about electronics; they really want that paycheck in their hands. But direct deposit is the absolute safest way to get their money into their bank account and the easiest way for you to help your parents manage their finances.

Bank Accounts

- *What's the name of the bank?* Remember: Don't assume the only bank account in use is the one tied to the checking and savings accounts. Your parent might have accounts at more than one bank, so be on the lookout for additional account statements, some of which might only arrive quarterly if the account is tied singularly to a certificate of deposit, or if the account is rarely accessed.

- *Which bank branch does your parent routinely visit?* Even if the bank account is held at a big national bank like Bank of America or Chase, the account statement will likely note the local branch where the account was opened. Assuming you are listed on the account or have power of attorney over your parent's finances— either of which will allow a bank manager to speak to you about your parent's account—visit that branch and determine whether Mom/Dad routinely deals with a particular bank employee. (To understand more about powers of attorney and why you need one when helping parent your parents, see page 51.) I keep an eye on the finances of my grandmother and her sister, my great-aunt, and the bank employee they always deal with— who knows I'm allowed to access the accounts—keeps me in the loop with what's happening in their accounts, or if either of them is having any sort of problem. For whatever reason, the elderly have a particular bond with their bankers, and those bankers, in turn, often have a good impression of how a parent is functioning, notice any changes in health or mental faculties, and can be a useful line of defense in alerting you to emerging issues, be they health related or possible anomalies in banking transactions.

- *What types of accounts are held at each bank and what are the account numbers?* Along with checking and savings accounts, certificates of deposit, and money market accounts, a parent could have a home equity loan or line of credit, a personal loan, a credit card, an individual retirement account, or some other asset or liability through their bank. Of particular note: Contact your parent's banker and ask if Mom/Dad happen to own a safe-deposit box at that particular bank. In many cases the elderly have simply forgotten they own a safe-deposit box, and thus have forgotten about all the documents and financial instruments and heirlooms they've stashed there. You will need either a power of attorney for this, or to head into the bank with Mom/Dad in tow and have your parent inquire on his or her own behalf.

- *How much money is in each account?* You'd be surprised how many retirees live like paupers but have a king's ransom stashed in bank accounts. Some live that way out of fear, some out of habit, and some because of psychological issues. Knowledge of the level of the assets inside bank accounts will help you to potentially redirect money into more productive uses for your parent, or can help you more easily cover the costs of a parent's needs when you're called in to run the finances.

- *Does your parent use online banking?* This is not something
  that will necessarily be part of the account statement. Instead, you'll have to ask Mom/Dad. If they do bank via
  the Internet, what are the log-in and password necessary
  for each account? Though a parent might be concerned
  about sharing this data, it's critical for you to know it so
  you can more easily oversee their finances by keeping
  track of income and spending, or by paying their bills electronically. If Mom/Dad doesn't use online banking, consider changing that. Online access to a parent's account,
  twenty-four hours a day, from any Internet-connected
  computer in the world will be immensely helpful.
- *Are there any direct deposits or automatic deductions?* Along with
  direct deposits for Social Security, pensions, or annuities,
  Mom/Dad might have other preauthorized transactions
  tied to the bank account. It could be that interest income
  from a CD is automatically dumped into the checking
  account instead of remaining in the CD account. Or possibly a regular insurance premium or some other payment is automatically deducted. You need to know the
  amount of the additions and subtractions. Examine each.
  Some will be clear, like the deposit of CD interest or
  the deduction of an insurance payment. Others that you
  don't recognize you need to question. And if your parent
  can't provide that answer then ask the bank to help you
  research it. It's possible Mom/Dad unwittingly agreed
  to an automatic electronic withdrawal and are receiving
  little or no services for the cost they're paying. Where
  direct deposits/automatic withdrawals exist, make note
  of the authorized amount, when the transaction typically
  occurs during the month (helpful for budgeting), and the

authorized debtor/creditor so that you can contact that company if necessary.

> **TIP:** Go through a recent checkbook register or several months of your parent's canceled checks to build a rough profile of typical expenses. This will not only help with budgeting by highlighting your parent's spending patterns, but it can reveal expenses in your parent's life that you might not have considered or that you might otherwise not recognize as a bill when it arrives in the mail. If Mom/Dad don't keep the registers, or if the bank doesn't return canceled checks, no worries. Use online access to the account to download past statements.

Brokerage Accounts, Mutual Funds, and Other Investment Account Statements

- *What's the name of the firm and what's the contact information?*
- *What type of financial services firm is this?* It could be a traditional full-service brokerage firm (Merrill Lynch, Edward Jones, Morgan Stanley, etc.); an online discount stockbroker (Charles Schwab & Co., E*Trade, Fidelity, Scottrade, and the like); a mutual funds company through which investors hold a standard account or often an **individual retirement account** (there are too many of these firms to list, though some of the most common providers are Vanguard and T. Rowe Price);

or, depending on how exotic your parent might have been as an investor, you might even find something like a **currency trading account** or an online bank account from an outfit like EverBank that holds certificates of deposit denominated in a foreign currency. If you're uncertain of what you're looking at, pull up the company on the Internet (I guarantee the firm will have a website), or call the listed phone number and ask.

- *What is the total value of the account?* This will be easy enough to find, and it will be obvious on the statement. You need this to tally the value of all your parent's assets, which represents the money you will be able to use to help Mom/Dad create the income they need to live on in retirement, or that you'll need to draw on to pay for services like home health care or assisted living or nursing home costs.

- *Is a specific broker assigned to the account?* This is generally only an issue if Mom/Dad is using a full-service brokerage firm such as Merrill Lynch, Edward Jones, or Morgan Stanley. Depending on the size of your parent's account, those firms will either assign a broker to your parents, or, more likely, Mom/Dad will have found the broker on their own. You'll want to jot down that person's name and contact information, or highlight it on the statement and keep it handy so that you can call and introduce yourself and explain your new role as your parent's financial gatekeeper. As part of the conversation, request that duplicates of all transactions in the account, as well as all account statements be sent to your address. This way you will be able to keep tabs on what's going on inside the account, which will help you spot questionable withdrawals or suspicious trading patterns, like unauthorized trades or the purchase of investments that are inappropriate for a retiree.

- *What's in the account?* This is important. If you're not up to speed on the various types of investment products that exist, or if the contents of the account leave you stupefied, then spend some time on the Internet deciphering what Mom/Dad own. **Stocks** and **bonds** will generally be pretty easy to pick out, since they'll be denoted as something like Coca-Cola or IBM or Microsoft. So, too, will a basic investment like a certificate of deposit (brokerage firms sell lots of those). What you really want to pay attention to are **mutual funds** and more complex investments like annuity contracts. Stockbrokers are notorious for dumping into older clients' accounts a mishmash of proprietary investments, often garbage. By that I mean brokers at times get paid bigger commissions to hawk in-house mutual funds and other such products, so you end up seeing a lot of investments in the account emblazoned with the firm's name. Ultimately you want to see investments in this account that fit your parent's needs. In most cases that will mean a fairly conservative account filled with well-known, dividend-paying **blue-chip stocks**, U.S. **government bonds**, high-quality **corporate bonds**, and maybe even some local **municipal bonds**; or if it's a mutual fund portfolio, you want to see broad-based, low-cost **index funds**, or if they're not index funds then high-quality mutual funds with a long history of outperforming their **benchmarks**. If you want to check out the quality of the mutual funds in your parent's account, or if you want to do some basic research on a stock, like finding out if it pays a **dividend** or not, go to Morningstar (www.morningstar.com). There you can research, for free, stocks, mutual funds, and **exchange-traded funds**. The data will show you how the funds' fee structures compare to the industry, how risky the fund is on a relative basis, and you can gauge each fund's past performance vs. whatever benchmark that fund targets. (A caveat: If Mom/Dad has an account at Fidelity or Vanguard and you see a lot of proprietary funds, that's not necessarily a cause for concern. These are generally self-directed brokerage accounts to begin with, and Fidelity and Vanguard dish up a large number of low-cost, quality funds.)

- Examine several months of statements and take note of the amount of trading taking place in the account. Elderly investors are not generally traders. They're much more the buy-and-hold type. Almost universally, they want solid, stable investments that are not risky and that pay them some level of income—again, big blue-chip stocks and government/corporate bonds. If you see a lot of trading activity from month to month, with quick darts into and out of individual stocks, or lots of transferring between mutual funds, you've got a problem. There's a strong likelihood the broker, or someone else overseeing the account, is "churning." That's when a broker buys and sells investments for the sole purpose of generating a commission for himself on each buy and sell transaction. Immediately contact the brokerage firm's corporate compliance department. Do not call the broker first and give him time to prepare a defense. Go to the compliance department and file a complaint, then file a complaint with the local securities regulator in your parents' state. You won't likely be able to reverse the trades, but you will probably end up in arbitration, where you will likely recoup some or all of the money your parents lost in the transactions and the costs they paid for the unnecessary trading.

TIP: Be on the lookout for an annuity held inside of an individual retirement account. This is a strong warning sign that your parent's broker is looking out for his own wallet instead of abiding by his fiduciary duty to act in your parent's best interest.

Not to get numbingly technical, but an annuity is a **tax deferred** investment product. And an IRA is a tax deferred investment account. In most instances, it makes little sense to hold a tax deferred investment inside a tax deferred account; there's no such thing as double tax deferral. Nevertheless, brokers often sell annuities into an older client's IRA because of the commission involved. Retirees will often accumulate a decent sum of money in an IRA through the years, or at retirement will transfer a lump sum of cash into an IRA from their company's **401(k) plan**. Brokers see that wad of cash as a money machine and look for the product that will generate the biggest payday, the biggest commission. That's often an annuity.

Thus, too often a retiree ends up with a tax deferred annuity inside a tax deferred IRA, and all they've managed to do is pay a broker big dollars for nothing. If you see this arrangement in your parent's IRA, press the broker intently to explain why such a belt-and-suspenders approach is appropriate for your parent, given that the financial community widely pans this strategy. And, in most cases, you might just go ahead and move the account to another broker in whom you have greater trust.

Dividend Reinvestment Plans

Many people participate in these so-called DRiPs, some tied to a former place of employment. These are essentially investments in which an investor owns shares of an individual dividend paying stock and has the dividends funneled back into—or reinvested in—that company's stock. For instance, your parent might own shares of Coca-Cola, and every quarter instead of receiving a dividend check in the mail, Mom/Dad receives a statement from Coke reporting the total value of the dividend and how many additional new Coke shares the dividend purchased. Here are some important points to look out for:

- *How many shares does Mom/Dad own, and what are the shares worth?* The statement will detail that for you in a summation that lays out "Total Shares Held" and "Total Value of Shares." The total number of shares held will be based on two factors: how many shares Mom/Dad own in physical form, and how many shares are held electronically by the underlying company's "stock transfer agent," the firm assigned to track who owns shares in the company and how many shares they own.

The shares held electronically do not exist physically; they are simply electronic notations representing the number of shares purchased into the account through the years from all the dividend payments received. The value of all the shares will likely be inaccurate at the moment you examine the statement, since that value will be based on the price of the stock on the day the statement was printed. By the time the statement arrives in the mailbox, the share price will almost assuredly be different. If you want or need to know the accurate value, then just multiply the total number of shares by the stock's current price, which you can do online very quickly at Google Finance (www.google .com/finance) or Yahoo! Finance (finance.yahoo.com). Or just type something like "Coca-Cola stock price" into a search engine and a link will pop up that will take you to the current price.

- *Where does your parent keep the physical share certificate?* Because DRiPs are not tied to a traditional brokerage account, the plans typically require that an investor own at least one share of stock, held in that investor's name. In practical terms, that means that if Mom/Dad participates in a DRiP, then a good chance exists that they own the physical shares of stocks somewhere, most likely a safe-deposit box at the bank or a lockbox in the house— though some investors might just file the shares away in a manila folder in the filing cabinet under the name of the company or maybe "DRiP." The quarterly statement will tell you if your parent owns physical shares. As noted in the previous bullet point, a DRiP statement will detail shares "Held by Us (Plan)" and "Held by You in

Certificate Form," or something along those lines. The "Held by You" tells you that physical certificates exist. If you ultimately cannot find those shares, and your parent can't remember where they might be, you can contact the company directly or its **transfer agent** and request a new certificate be issued. The statement will give you all the contact information. Though it takes some effort, lost certificates can be replaced fairly easily.

- *How many DRiPs do Mom/Dad participate in?* Parents can belong to more than one DRiP, and each has its separate statement. Each DRiP is specific to a single company, and companies do not aggregate their individual plans on a single statement. So where a parent might own ten or twelve stocks at a brokerage firm, all of which are cataloged on one monthly statement, with DRiPs your parent would have ten or twelve individual statements arriving every quarter. (Most dividends are paid quarterly, and the account statements are dispatched only when there's activity in the account. And because companies pay their dividends on their own schedule, the account statements will arrive at various times during the quarter, rather than all at once.)

With most financial statements, particularly bank account statements, there's no need to keep anything other than the most recent statement. With DRiPs, however, you *must* keep every one that arrives. The reason: Each statement details the cost basis of the shares being purchased with that quarter's dividend payment. This is crucial information if you or your parent must sell the stock to meet financial needs while Mom/Dad is still alive. Tax calculations require that you determine the profit and loss for each transaction. Thus, you'll need to know that the 1.046 shares of some company purchased into the account in January 1992 had a cost basis of $10.96. With a lot of effort, you can probably rebuild the account history with the help of the company or its transfer agent, but that will be cumbersome.

TIP: Keep a file for every DRiP statement that arrives. If, however, the shares aren't sold until after a parent's death, then the original cost basis might be moot—the emphasis on "might be." Tax laws, as they existed in 2010, allowed for a so-called step-up in basis when the owner dies and bequeaths shares of stock to an heir or an estate. An estate's executor has the right to effectively assign to heirs the stock at a cost equal to the market value of those shares on the date of your parent's death. In practical terms that means, for instance, that if Mom/Dad owned shares of Coca-Cola at an original cost of $5,000, and those shares are worth $50,000 when the parent dies, the heir gets the stock at an adjusted cost of $50,000, bypassing taxes that might otherwise be due on the $45,000 in underlying profits. When the shares are ultimately sold, taxes will be due on any profits that accrue above the $50,000 basis. As of this writing, the step-up basis can wipe out up to $1.3 million in stock market appreciation, but remember that we are dealing with Congress; lawmakers desperate to corral additional monies on which to run a bloated government are always capable of fiddling with this rule in ways that do not benefit heirs. So always check with a tax or estate attorney to make sure no changes have occurred since this was written.

Credit Card Statements

- *What's the name of the credit card company?* With all the affinity marketing going on these days, the name of the card provider might not be readily apparent from what's printed on the front of the card. Flip it over and examine the back. There you'll find the name of the underlying company—and it will probably be Bank of America, Citibank, or Capital One. Others that will be more obvious are American Express and Discover. You will also probably find a gas card or two tied to one of the major petroleum companies, like ExxonMobil, Shell, Texaco, BP, etc. And you can probably bet on some local store-brand charge cards like Sears. Note, as well, the account number and the company's contact information.

TIP: Obtain a free copy of Mom/Dad's credit report, and if both parents are still alive, get the credit reports for both of them. Here's why: It will detail for you every single credit card, loan, and mortgage that exists in a parent's name. This will help you unearth debts you didn't know about, or discover credit cards that are floating around that a parent hasn't used in years and has no need for anymore. Moreover, it can help you determine if a maid, home health worker, or someone else has usurped a parent's identity and is racking up debts in your parent's name. The elderly are especially susceptible to ID theft, and are slow to catch on because they're not always interacting in the arenas where they'd typically uncover the crime. You can obtain Mom/Dad's credit report every year for

free by going to www.annualcreditreport.com, operated by the
three major credit reporting agencies. You'll have collected the
information you'll need to obtain the report during The Talk.

- *Does Mom/Dad have online access to the credit card account?*
  If so, you'll need their log-in and password so you can
  manage the account as necessary. If Mom/Dad don't
  access credit card statements online, then set that up
  yourself, since, as with banking, dealing with issues that
  arise or tracking spending will be far more convenient
  for you if you can pull up the account any time of day
  and from any Internet-connected computer.
- *What are the names on the account?* Is this held in just one
  parent's name, or both? Or is there someone else's name
  on the account that you don't recognize? And though
  some people feel compelled to put their own name on a
  parent's credit card, or to open a joint credit card with
  their parents in order to better manage the account,
  don't. This becomes a liability for you. If for whatever
  reason your parent accumulates a huge debt on this card
  or without your knowledge rolls the balance of ten other
  credit cards onto this new card, you are suddenly on
  the hook for as much as half of the balance, even if you
  had nothing to do with amassing that balance. There are
  savvier ways to help your parent manage credit cards,
  often by simply gaining access to the account online so
  that you can keep tabs on spending and repayments, and
  by helping Mom/Dad more effectively use their budget
  to extinguish the debt.

- *What's the outstanding balance?* The "minimum balance due" is effectively a useless number, since it is designed to pay off even a relatively small debt over an extended period of years, in the process accumulating big profits for the credit card company at the expense of the cardholder. (For instance, a debt of $1,200 on a card that charges 19% interest and imposes a minimum balance due each month of $31, would take 133 months, or just over eleven years, to completely pay off the balance. And with principal and interest your parent will have paid a total of $2,506, more than double the original debt.) Thus, what you want to pay attention to is how much money is due overall, so that you can begin to work these debts into Mom/Dad's monthly budget and pay them off quicker by doubling, or tripling the minimum due, or paying it down in big chunks.

- *What is the interest rate?* This goes hand in hand with the balance. The higher the rate is, the larger the interest that is due on the outstanding balance. You will find the interest rate spelled out on the back of the statement. Compare the rate your parent is paying to the national average detailed at www.bankrate.com. And if Mom/Dad has multiple cards with a balance, simplify your life and theirs by combining those balances onto a single, low-rate card. If your parent already has a card with a particularly low rate, combine the other balances onto that card. If all the cards carry onerous rates, then hit the Internet to research low-rate credit cards at either Bankrate.com or CardTrak.com (www.cardtrak.com), an independent source that for years has provided *The*

Wall Street Journal with the credit card rate data it publishes monthly. In a situation where combining balances would put a parent at or above the card's existing credit limit, call the card company and request a credit limit increase, explaining what you're trying to accomplish for your parent. You will either need Mom/Dad on the phone with you to give the card company permission to talk to you, or you'll need to send the company a copy of the power of attorney that gives you control over the account.

Insurance Policies

- *What is the name and contact information for the insurer and the policy number?* In terms of contact information, you'll want the phone number and address for the company on a national or regional level, as well as the name and phone number of the local agent, which should be on the premium notice somewhere.

- *What type of policy is this?* The most common policies are those covering life, health, auto, and home. Some parents with a higher level of assets might also have an umbrella policy providing $1 million or $2 million that in blanket fashion provides coverage in the event Mom/Dad is sued for causing substantial damages or death to another person, often the result of an auto accident. Others might have a long-term care policy to provide coverage for the expenses of a nursing home, assisted living center, or home health aide, among other costs.

- *How much does the policy cost?* This is the so-called premium. You'll need this as part of the upcoming budgeting process. Note if the premium is automatically deducted from a checking or savings account, and if it is you'll want to monitor that account to ensure it maintains enough money to pay the premium, otherwise there's a risk that the premium goes unpaid and the policy gets canceled. In the case of long-term care policies, those premiums are often paid quarterly, but budgeting is generally a monthly process. As such, you'll want to divide the quarterly premium by three so that your parent's budget adequately reflects the accurate monthly costs and so that the account has enough cash in it to pay the premium when the notice arrives.

- *What does the policy cover?* The elderly often don't realize what their insurance covers. My great-aunt, in presenting me with all her end-of-life paperwork and financial documents, showed me an insurance policy that she said would pay out $10,000 upon her death. I looked it over and realized it was an "accidental death" policy she'd bought years ago from her employer's list of group insurance policies. I explained to her that the policy would only pay out in the event she dies while in an airplane crash, an auto accident, or maybe if she gets conked on the head with a golf ball while out on the course. She vehemently disagreed. I told her to call the insurer and ask if the policy would pay a death benefit if she died of natural causes or because of a heart attack or cancer or whatnot. She sheepishly called me two days later and said I was right, that she had canceled the contract, and that she was angry she'd spent all the money through the years on something she didn't need or want. The message: Read through the policy's coverage to determine what it does—and doesn't—cover, and ask if that's what your parent really wants or needs. The premium notice for some policies will include a so-called declarations page, or the "dec," which explicitly spells out the coverage. Other times you will either have to root through your parent's files to find the contract or call the insurer to request a copy of the dec. This is yet another instance where you will likely need the power of attorney to obtain the information from the insurer.

- *With life insurance and long-term care policies, what are the total benefits?* Life insurance pays out a so-called death benefit, which is sometimes detailed on the premium notice but is always included on an annual policy summary mailed to the policyholder (find it in your parent's file or call the insurer). **Term life** policies pay a predetermined benefit—such as $50,000, $100,000, etc.—and they automatically lapse after a predetermined number of years, often ten or twenty. **Permanent life** policies such as whole life and universal life contracts have a variety of payout possibilities. These policies operate in dual fashion. First, they function just like a term life policy in that they pay a death benefit. Second, they function like an investment/savings account, accumulating additional financial benefits over time, depending on the performance of an underlying investment/savings subaccount. Accordingly, these policies are ones from which a parent might be able to borrow money to meet financial needs. Because permanent life policies can be so complex and so varied, you need to meet with the agent who sold the policy, or the insurance company behind the policy, to understand exactly what Mom/Dad owns, whether the coverage is still necessary, and to determine how much the policy is worth in the event your parent wants to cash it in to pay for other costs. As for long-term care, there is a big section on it coming up in chapter 6, "The Health."

Mortgage Statements, Home Equity Lines of Credit, Home Equity Loans, Second Mortgages, Reverse Mortgages, Auto Loans, and Auto Leases

- *What's the name of each lender, and the contact information?*
- *What are the account numbers?*
- *What's the size of the account balance and what is the monthly payment?* The payments, in particular, will help with budgeting, while the account balances will help you structure a debt-repayment plan, in which you begin to funnel some portion of your parent's income into additional **principal** repayment. This repayment is generally geared toward **home equity loans, home equity lines of credit,** and **second mortgages**. It is not an issue with **reverse mortgages,** since those are handled much differently (more on reverse mortgages later).
- *What are the interest rates charged on each outstanding balance?* Elderly parents, in particular, don't always pay attention to interest rates; they are focused instead on the

affordability of the monthly payment. Pay attention, instead, to the interest rate your parent is paying and compare it to prevailing rates. You might find that refinancing the existing debt at lower prevailing rates will sharply reduce your parent's monthly obligations, freeing up additional spendable income.

• *Are the rates fixed or variable?* For the elderly, **fixed rate debt** is generally a much better option than **variable rate debt**. The reason: The elderly typically live on a fixed income, so their obligations should be equally fixed, if possible. You don't want to find Mom/Dad stuck in a situation where large debt on a mortgage or home loan is suddenly skyrocketing amid a surge in interest rates. That will cause monthly payments to push higher, possibly at such a pace and to such a degree that your parent's monthly income can no longer cover the payment and adequately provide for all the other necessary expenses. If you find your parent does have a loan or mortgage with a variable rate, you should shop around with local and online banks and lenders to find a suitable fixed rate replacement and refinance the debt. To get an idea of prevailing rates on mortgage and home equity loans, check in with Bankrate.com. There you will also find various calculators that will help you determine whether it makes sense to refinance the debt, and will calculate the potential savings.

Electricity, Gas, Water, Heating Oil, Telephone, and Internet Bills

- *What's the contact information?* The name and contact information for each provider is generally the only information you need to know, since you may need to call these providers to sort out any problems that crop up.
- *How do you find the best deal for your parents?* The balance due will give you a plot point you can use for budgeting, but many of these services will fluctuate from month to month, season to season. Monthly Internet bills, if your parent uses the Internet, are generally fixed. With some of the core utilities providers, like gas and electric, you can request your parent be put on a plan that effectively averages a homeowner's utility consumption over the course of a year, and then bills that amount at a fixed price every month. In some places, competition is fierce and consumers can shop around for electricity providers who offer the best deal, though that means Mom/Dad will likely have to lock into a one- or two-year contract. Nevertheless, this can be an effective way of reducing monthly expenses. Utility providers can also point you toward local or national organizations that offer financial assistance in helping older homeowners make their houses more energy efficient, which in turn will reduce electricity costs.
- *Can you become a secondary contact?* Reach out to each provider and add your information to the account as an emergency/secondary contact, if the provider will allow that. This way, if a problem ever emerges, you will be

called to address it before the service is shut off—a particularly useful service if you and your parent live in different cities.

Subscriptions

• *What publications does your parent receive?* Pay attention to the newspapers and magazines that arrive daily or that accumulate in your parent's house. Do they look like they've been digested, or do they look unread? Telemarketers pitching magazine and newspaper subscriptions routinely prey on older folks. And the elderly often return mailers subscribing to some periodical that seemed interesting in the moment, but that they no longer read or want. Some are just kindly to the neighborhood children who come by trying to sell subscriptions for various charitable causes. I stopped by to visit my grandmother one Saturday afternoon and I noticed she had several copies of *Rolling Stone* magazine on her coffee table, and the information on the cover showed that she was a subscriber. My grandmother is eighty-nine. She wouldn't know the Doobie Brothers from the Righteous Brothers from the Jonas Brothers. Clearly, some telemarketer convinced her to subscribe to a publication for which she has zero use. Thus, this is an area where you can find some savings. Cancel the subscriptions that are unread and request a reimbursement of the unused portion.

- *When keeping a subscription, what is the cost and how often is it billed?* Even a bill for $35 for a subscription to some magazine can cause a budgetary headache for a parent with a limited income. Better to plan these expenses, even if they're small, so that when they arrive the outlay doesn't put a strain on a parent's ability to pay for more important costs.

- *When canceling subscriptions, ask,"Is this subscription on automatic renew?"* Often newspaper and magazine subscriptions automatically renew until the subscriber explicitly says to stop. That means Mom/Dad's bank account or credit card is automatically drafted each month, or every quarter or every year. You need to explicitly ask the subscription provider if the current subscription is on auto-renew, and if so to cancel that, too.

- Remember: Subscriptions aren't just reading material. Your parent might have subscribed to a movie service like Netflix, get billed monthly on the credit card, but never rent the movies. It might even be a cheese of the month club. Pay attention to the credit card bill each month, where these kinds of charges typically congregate.

TIP: With financial and insurance accounts, call each company and ask whether your parent has named a **beneficiary** and, if so, whom. Request a copy of the document that names the beneficiary; often it will also offer details such as the address and/or Social Security number of the beneficiary, which can be helpful in instances when you might not know the person and might want to make contact in order to determine why this person is in line to benefit from your parent's insurance policies or financial accounts. This is yet another instance where a power of attorney is necessary before a firm releases the information.

But it can be crucial information. Many times a parent either hasn't named a beneficiary or has listed a beneficiary who has already died. Both cases can cause inheritance headaches or even intrafamily fisticuffs if there have been marriages and divorces and remarriages. Other times you might discover a beneficiary is named who you've never heard of; this could be your indication that foul play is at hand, since con artists posing as friends and confidants worm their way into an elderly person's life and manipulate the situation to have themselves listed as beneficiaries of insurance policies, financial accounts, or even a house.

Long-Range Documents

THESE ARE DOCUMENTS YOUR parent needs for long-range financial, inheritance, or end-of-life planning, or that will simply bestow on you—or someone else—the power to act on Mom/Dad's behalf when necessary.

In the context of long-range documents and the need to step into a parent's life, perhaps the biggest issue you will potentially confront in a very broad sense is that of **guardianship**, or **conservatorship**, as it's known in some states. Guardians/conservators are appointed by the courts to make personal/financial decisions for another person who the court determines is incapable of making those decisions independently. Adult children often seek guardianship when Mom/ Dad clearly isn't keeping up with routine personal financial decisions or is making decisions that do not reflect prudence or past financial patterns.

In such a situation, seeking guardianship over an aging parent can make sense. It might be the only option available in cases in which Mom/Dad is belligerent or defiant in spurning your attempts to help, but where you recognize that without someone stepping in Mom/Dad faces dire financial consequences.

But do not rush toward guardian/conservator status without strong cause. Guardianship means severe deprivation of your parent's right to make decisions, and that can result in emotional strains that take a toll on your own well-being.

Guardianship/conservatorship requires a legal hearing to determine the competency of your parent, and may require the evaluation of psychiatrists and social workers, among others. If the court determines a parent cannot make informed decisions, or is a menace to their own financial security, the court can appoint a guardian/conservator—but there is no guarantee you will be the one selected. And if you are selected, the court can require that you submit regular reports to ensure that you are not abusing your power.

Before pursuing guardianship, consider other legal options that can provide the same end results—you helping manage end-of-life issues—without stepping on a parent's right to self-determination.

We'll start with the durable power of attorney.

Durable Power of Attorney

- *What it is:* A durable power of attorney is a legal document that grants a specified person the right to make decisions for your parent. In other words, your parent signs a power of attorney that gives to you, or to another designated person, the right to act on your parent's behalf. That makes a durable power of attorney one of the most useful and necessary documents for helping manage a parent's life. The document will allow you great dominion in handling and finalizing various legal contracts and financial transactions that will become necessary as Mom/Dad age.

- *What it covers:* Powers of attorney can be structured to grant authority over limited circumstances, or to cover the full scope of a parent's life. Equally important is the distinction between a "durable" and a traditional power of attorney. The durable version continues after a parent is incapacitated, which makes them of greater utility when you're dealing with eldercare and end-of-life issues.

- *What it doesn't allow:* A durable power of attorney is limited by what the document explicitly covers. If oversight of a particular account or a particular component of your parent's life is not defined in the document, then that power isn't conveyed.

- *When the powers kick in:* Powers of attorney can be written so that they come into force immediately, giving you authority to act on your parent's behalf when the document is signed, or they can be "springing" versions that take effect upon the emergence of a specific event, such as a parent's incapacitation. How Mom/Dad chooses to structure the document depends on personal wants. The springing version is best used for situations in which Mom/Dad do not want to grant wide-ranging authority over their life immediately, but do want that power to arise when they become incapable of managing their affairs.

A note of caution: When your parent elects a springing power of attorney, encourage Mom/Dad to define explicitly their definition of "incapacitated"—maybe something like, "incapacitated as determined by a doctor who declares I am no longer capable of caring for my daily needs or managing my finances." After all, the term "incapacity" is a broad, nebulous term, and a parent's version might differ sharply from yours or whomever Mom/Dad selected to hold the power of attorney. This decision should include consultation with a lawyer or eldercare attorney who is familiar with this situation.

Durable Power of Attorney for Health Care

- *What it is:* This is similar to the durable power of attorney, but it pertains specifically to health care decisions that must be made on behalf of an incapacitated parent. The document is also known as a "health care power of attorney" or a "health care proxy."
- *What it covers:* This document exclusively deals with medical decisions. Whoever your parent names will have the authority to tell doctors what to do—and what not to do.

- *When it kicks in:* This document takes effect when a parent is physically or mentally incapable of making necessary medical decisions. For that reason, you, or whoever will be called on to stand in, need to have a discussion with Mom/Dad to clearly understand wishes and wants. Similarly, a parent needs to structure the document to explicitly state certain desires, such as not being kept alive in a "persistent vegetative state," or even religious objections to certain medical treatments or procedures.

Living Will

- *What it is:* A living will is a written declaration that directs a doctor or other health care professional in the use of life-sustaining medical treatments when the lack of treatment would mean death. These are also known as an "advance directive," "health care directive," or "physician's directive."
- *What it covers:* A living will exclusively focuses on life-sustaining medical treatments, not routine health care issues, which are covered by the health care power of attorney. In essence, we're talking about terminal illnesses for which treatment will not provide a cure, though it would likely maintain life in a permanent, unconscious state.
- *When it kicks in:* A living will only takes effect when life-sustaining medical treatment is required but would only postpone the moment of death, or would maintain a permanent, vegetative state. In these situations, the living will tells doctors how to proceed, based on your parent's wishes. Through the document, parents

define the kinds of treatments they specifically do not want. So, for instance, if Mom/Dad do not want to be kept alive artificially if there's no hope for a return to a quality state of living, then a living will spells that out and a physician would abide by those dictates, even if Mom/Dad have no ability to voice those wishes at that moment. Before the mandates of the living will kick in, though, your parent's doctor and often a second doctor must certify that Mom/Dad is suffering from a terminal illness for which there is no hope for recovery.

- Because laws vary by state, counsel your parents to use a lawyer who is familiar with drafting living wills where your parents reside.

TIP: Health care power of attorney or living will—which does your parent need?

The two documents are similar in scope, yet the durable health care power of attorney is a broader, more flexible document. So if you're going to encourage your parents to choose one—assuming Mom/Dad doesn't already have one—then push for the power of attorney.

The health care power of attorney can cover all the same bases the living will covers, yet the power of attorney is not limited to situations in which your parent is dealing with a terminal illness or life-threatening injury. And Mom/Dad can effectively combine living will wishes into a power of attorney. This way you and your parent's health care provider are working from a single document rather than two that could contradict one another unintentionally depending on who drew them up and when they were drawn up, and then it's a potential fight to determine which document rules the day.

HIPAA Authorization

- *What it is:* The federal Health Insurance Portability and Accountability Act of 1996 is a law that among other requirements mandates that medical services providers protect patient data. That means even if you are acting on behalf of a parent, you can't just walk into a doctor's office and have a discussion about Mom/Dad's cholesterol level. HIPAA laws won't allow that. To provide for that, your parent needs to sign a HIPAA authorization that explicitly allows you, or whomever your parent designates, to gain access to health care data and information.

- *What it covers:* HIPAA laws apply to health care providers, pharmacies, nursing homes, hospitals, insurance companies, and just about any other medical care provider or organization you can conjure. Protected information includes documents or charts related to physical or mental condition or the health services provided that could identify a patient. Thus, the HIPAA authorization is necessary when dealing with any of these entities on behalf of Mom/Dad.

- *When it kicks in:* Anytime you approach a health-related entity on behalf of Mom/Dad, a HIPAA authorization is required.

- *How HIPAA differs from health care power of attorney:* In some ways the power of attorney and a HIPAA authorization overlap one another, and a power of attorney can be written to include HIPAA language. But in one crucial aspect they can differ. If the power of attorney is structured to take effect when a parent becomes incapacitated, then it does no good under normal circumstances when you might need to act as your parent's agent in a situation where Mom/Dad is not incapacitated. If your parent hasn't already signed a HIPAA authorization, then this is a crucial issue that needs to be addressed.

Revocable Living Trust

- *What it is:* A revocable living trust is a written agreement that designates a trustee to be responsible for managing "property" on behalf of another person while that other person is alive though incapacitated. As the name implies, this trust is revocable, meaning a parent—so long as he or she remains mentally competent—can change the terms of the trust, can alter what it covers, can name a new trustee, new beneficiaries, or end the trust entirely.

- *What it covers:* In the context of a living trust, property defines assets such as land, cash, investments, rental property, buildings, and the like. That's where it differs from a **living will**; the living will caters to medical issues, while the **living trust** centers on property. The named trustee manages this property based on Mom/Dad's wishes, as defined by the trust. In many cases, the person forming the trust leaves it empty until a predetermined moment, such as incapacity. That allows a parent to maintain full control over property and assets and only relinquish that control to a trustee at the moment Mom/Dad can no longer manage the property.

- *Who it's right for:* Not every parent will need a revocable living trust. The need depends on the assets; if Mom/Dad has assets that need to be managed, then a living trust is probably a worthy document. If they have no real assets to speak of, then there's likely no need for one. After you build a profile of the assets and property that your parents own, talk to an estate planning attorney to gauge the need for a trust.

Will

- *What it is:* A will is a legally binding document that spells out how property should be distributed after death. If Mom/Dad don't draw up a will prior to death, then asset distribution will fall to the state—and how the state divvies up property might not match your parent's wishes. That makes a will possibly the most important estate planning document.
- *What it covers:* It covers anything from cash to collectible baseball cards to an old collection of family recipes. A parent determines what to leave to whom, and spells that out explicitly in the will. Upon death, the courts generally abide by those wishes—although there's always the chance that someone contests the will and forces a legal battle over where an asset should rightfully go.
- *Who needs one:* Anyone who owns any sort of asset, or who has underage children, needs a will.
- Wills do not need to be complex. A basic will is plenty,

so long as the document is witnessed. These can be handwritten or typed, or produced inexpensively with computer software that asks all the pertinent questions and then spits out a basic will. This no-nonsense will is particularly useful and convenient in situations where siblings won't attack one another in court fighting over who gets what, where there's little or no chance someone will claim the document is fraudulent, or where the combined value of your parent's assets isn't likely to be subject to estate taxes. (Estate tax thresholds are in flux as of this writing in 2010, so you'll need to gauge where the tax threshold begins at the time you're dealing with this issue with your parents.) On the other hand, your parents likely need the help of a lawyer to fashion a comprehensive will if they: own assets that clearly will incur estate taxes; want to control from the grave how certain assets are managed for, say, a special-needs child or for some other reason; or in cases where there have been multiple marriages and there's a chance that nonrelated offspring will devolve into bickering and court fights.

TIP: If you or your parents don't have enough money for a local attorney to draft the necessary documents, go online and you will find a variety of websites that offer free legal forms or affordable legal software. You just plug in the data the form requests, and the website or software cranks out a standard document. Just be certain that the documents are valid in whatever state your parent resides, and be aware of the fact that the documents you produce might need to be notarized.

Also note that some legal programs do not work in some states. For instance, Louisiana's civil law system, which is based largely on Napoleonic code, differs from the common-law doctrines of the other forty-nine states, and thus not many legal software programs are set up to account for the various differences that exist.

If you have no interest in the do-it-yourself route, contact local organizations that cater to eldercare issues, such as the Area Agency on Aging. These organizations will be able to point you toward local attorneys who do pro bono work with the elderly. Plug the name of your parent's town and "Area Agency on Aging" into your favorite Web browser and the local contact information will pop up.

3

The Money, Part 1

Banking and Budgeting

PARENTS CAN BE HAZARDOUS to their own wealth. The real problems for you arise when that hazard explodes into your life, often unexpectedly. The cleanup can be a torrential headache, consuming weeks and months of your time, and possibly hundreds or thousands of your own dollars.

Consider this very real example a longtime acquaintance shared with me: He had traveled to a Sun Belt state for a long holiday weekend with Mom and Dad only to learn while visiting that his retired parents had accumulated some $60,000 in debt on multiple credit cards. The combined minimum payments were consuming nearly all of their monthly retirement income. He came to discover they'd been living well beyond their means for years, funding vacations, meals, groceries, presents, and a litany of other expenses with credit cards, then allowing the balance to roll over from month to month, accumulating thousands of dollars in interest along the way. The "minimum due" line grew larger and larger until it reached a point where the amount was nearly equal to their total monthly income.

My friend immediately grasped the gravity of their situation and ultimately forced his parents to pursue bankruptcy—though success on that front meant weeks of negotiating with them and explaining in stark detail that they really had no other viable alternatives.

Certainly not all parents will find themselves in such a quagmire. Many managed their money prudently throughout life, and continue to do so in their latter years. Yet just because a financial calamity hasn't befallen your parents doesn't mean you can check "money worries" off your list. Even in the best of financial situations, you need at least a rudimentary understanding of your parent's finances in the event you are called upon to take the reins in an emergency, or if your parent calls upon you to take control for any other reason.

This chapter, then, aims to help you navigate parental finances. Ultimately this is the core of the book, since money plays a primary role in just about every decision you and your parents must make about their lives—from where they live, to the health care they can afford, to the needs and wants they can fund in their monthly budget, to the inheritance they hope to one day leave to children, grandchildren, or charity.

You might think that your parents don't really have enough money to worry with in the first place. They might have lived a paycheck-to-paycheck, workaday lifestyle while raising you, and you just assume from outward appearances that their finances remain in roughly the same shape today. Maybe you're right. But that doesn't mean you should be complacent about the situation; parents with meager finances often need the most help managing what they do have and learning to better utilize their resources.

Or you might be wrong. Could be that your parents turn

up with a nest egg you or they never imagined because of company pensions, individual retirement accounts, lump-sum distributions from employer-sponsored retirement savings plans, and the equity in their home. That in itself could be problematic for parents who never had to manage such a sum when they were working and suddenly feel overwhelmed trying to do so late in life. In some situations, parents feel so flush with cash when they come into all this money upon retirement that they spend foolishly, thinking they can afford more than they really can and raising the risk that their money runs out long before their oxygen.

So once you've had The Talk and you've accumulated The Documents, your next move, before you can begin to address the other issues your parents might face, is to get a handle on Mom/Dad's financial situation. You need to know where the money is located; how it's allocated or invested; who, if anyone, is managing the money; how much money is coming in and from what sources; and what options exist for helping parents generate potentially more—and potentially permanent—income from the assets that exist.

We'll begin at the base of the financial pyramid: banking.

Banking

THE BASIC BANK ACCOUNT is in most instances the hub of your parent's financial activities. And the checkbook register is chock-full of information revealing important data on income, spending patterns, and, potentially, fraud being perpetrated against a parent. The register is effectively a personal financial diary that can expose a lot of what you want to know.

But unless a parent is clearly incapacitated—and that means medically diagnosed as such, not just your off-the-cuff judgment—you can't just go hunt for and scrutinize the checkbook register without a parent's prior approval. Technically, you *can*, of course, but you shouldn't. Remember, assisting Mom and Dad with their finances is, as best as it can be, an exercise in cooperation and communication. If you overstep your authority, usurp power, or are caught slinking around your parent's money affairs, you will, at best, create a great deal of anger and animosity that could destroy the trust a parent places in you. At worst, a spiteful parent can press charges against you, claiming elder abuse, particularly if you're caught monkeying around with their money. (More on financial elder abuse in a chapter 4.)

Before trying to collect all the banking information relevant to your parent's life, a conversation with Mom or Dad or both is necessary. In some instances, parents might approach you first, recognizing on their own that they need help managing their money or that they just want a sharper pair of eyes and sensibilities overseeing what transpires in their life financially. In other instances, starting the conversation is up to you. So, just as with The Talk, approach it honestly by offering your parents the opportunity to chat, if they want to, or at the very least planting the seed that they can act on later:

CONVERSATION STARTER

"Mom/Dad, I'm not trying to intrude on your personal financial affairs, but I just want you to know that I'm available if you need me to help you deal with any kind of banking or investment or budgeting issues."

To shape the context of your request, and to get your parents thinking beyond the highly personal nature of your comment, make the point as well that in any sort of emergency there are certain pieces of information regarding bank/investment accounts, sources of income, and debt obligations you're going to need to know about in order to adequately help them manage whatever event emerges. Again, no pressure. High-pressure situations are more likely to cause parents to shut down rather than open up, particularly when talking about their money. Leave the timeline to them. If Mom or Dad want to talk now, that's great. If you clearly sense their discomfort, offer reassurance that this topic needn't be addressed immediately, and that you're ready to talk whenever they are—and leave it at that. They'll call when the time is right. But don't let the issue just fade away. If need be, remind them of your interest from time to time, continually reiterating that you want to be as effective as possible if you're ever called on to help, and that at the end of the day you must know what you're dealing with in order to make their life easier when inconvenient moments arise.

TIP: Simplify. Through the years all of us accumulate a litany of accounts: multiple credit cards, multiple back accounts, multiple retirement savings accounts. To make it easier on you when taking charge of your parent's finances, consolidate each of those into a single account so that your parents have one credit card (assuming they still need one), one bank (though it might have multiple accounts for savings, checking, money market, etc.), and one individual retirement account.

You can consolidate IRAs a couple of ways. You can pick one of the accounts that currently exists and that is most convenient for you to manage, and then request that other bank and brokerage firms that hold IRA assets in your parent's name transfer those assets into the consolidating IRA. Or you can open a new IRA for your parents at the bank where their savings and checking assets are held, and have the other IRAs transferred into that new account. Don't forget that you can also transfer 401(k) plans and similar retirement savings accounts into a consolidating IRA as well, assuming that doing so makes sense for your parent.

A key question to address at some point in this banking conversation is whether you should be listed on their accounts with them.

While parents might initially have concerns about giving you implicit rights to their money, good reasons exist for sharing their account with you. Possibly the best reasons: You will have authority to tap into their account on their behalf in an emergency, while in nonemergency situations you will be able to assist them with financial problems that might emerge like misdirected payments from Social Security or a pension.

Several types of joint accounts exist, but the two most relevant to managing your parent's finances are joint tenants with rights of survivorship and tenants in common.

- *Rights of Survivorship*: When the last parent listed on the account dies, ownership of all assets in the account transfers to the surviving account holder.
- *Tenants in Common*: When the last parent listed on the account dies, assets pass to any heirs through a will or

through rules associated with intestacy (when a person dies without having made a valid will).

Which arrangement is right for your family is a complex question best addressed by an attorney or a tax professional in your particular state, since there are legal and tax considerations that come into play.

Generally speaking, if you're an only child, then rights of survivorship is likely the most efficient arrangement since the account will revert to your ownership without having to pass through a will or probate. But if you have siblings, then tenants in common is probably the better option since the remaining account assets reverting to your ownership could foul up estate planning, go against the desires expressed in the will, or cause a rift between you and your siblings. Again, check with a local attorney to be sure the account is structured properly.

If you do have siblings, refrain from putting your name on one account and a sibling's name on another account. You potentially create a conflicted situation in which you and the sibling end up fighting over the management of your parent's funds. Better for one sibling to manage the finances and, if necessary, keep the other sibling in the loop.

TIP: No matter how you ultimately structure your parent's accounts, keep meticulous records of *all* your activities in any account you have access to. Records serve as proof of what has transpired and can insulate you from legal action inspired by an angry sibling. Regularly share with siblings any copies of account statements so that they feel comfortable with your management. If a sibling is managing the money, require regular copies of account statements and that the sibling keeps meticulous records that you can examine and reconcile against those accounts when necessary.

What Assets Are in Mom/Dad's Bank Account?

The elderly tend to place a great deal of trust in their bankers. Too often it's misplaced trust because banks, in seeking ever more ways to generate income, have a nasty habit of exploiting their customers by pitching unsuitable and typically expensive products. That's a particular concern with older savers who generally assume the Federal Deposit Insurance Corporation insures all products sold within a bank, even though FDIC coverage is not universal.

In one high-profile case in Massachusetts in the mid-2000s, the state fined several banks for their concerted efforts at cold-calling seniors over the age of seventy-five and trying to convince each customer to move money out of staid certificates of deposit and into so-called **variable annuities**. CDs are typically a very good place for the elderly to park their money, though the idle cash doesn't much help banks. Variable annuities, meanwhile, are often an atrocious investment for the elderly, though the products earn big fees for the banks. Massachusetts's secretary of state at the time noted that one bank in particular was "deliberately targeting elderly customers" and that employees disregarded policies that require banks to ensure that products are suitable to an older customer's needs. The employees who sold the largest dollar amount of annuities were awarded company-paid trips to the Caribbean, while the insurance companies marketing the annuities offered free tickets to concerts and sporting events and trips to casinos and golf resorts.

These types of shenanigans are more common than you might imagine, and regulators routinely reprimand and fine banks for inappropriately pitching risky products to the elderly. Banks these days often own investment arms and though it borders on the shady, many mine their list of banking clients, trolling for those with large balances sitting in a savings or money market account, and then share that information with the brokerage side of the business, aiming to push those funds into products that earn more fees for the bank. Some banks go so far as to phone customers with heavy balances, imply there's a problem with the account, and then urge the elderly client to hurry in to the branch to reconcile this issue. There the customer learns the "problem" is that the account is underperforming its earning power by sitting idle in a savings account or money market account, and that the solution to this financial calamity is any of a list of other products ranging from personalized **wealth management** to insurance contracts to an annuity (a bigger section on annuities is forthcoming).

As such, when compiling the list of your parent's bank accounts, scrutinize any account that goes beyond the traditional checking, savings, **money market**, or certificate of deposit. Question the bank's manager, the person who sold the product, or some bank representative other than the teller. Seek a rationale for why the bank determined your parent needed this product. Ask about fees or charges imposed to exit the product early. And ask how much the agent earned in a commission. If the answer is "nothing," there's an excellent chance the salesperson is lying. All financial products compensate the seller in some fashion, otherwise the seller would have little incentive to pitch that product. So press hard on that issue and ask about **back-end fees** or **trailing commissions** the agent earns from the financial services company behind whatever it is your parent bought.

If you are dissatisfied with the answer, request that the transaction be reversed, and remind the agent, the branch manager, and the bank's home office that state and federal investment laws require banks to abide by **"know your customer"** rules and to offer investment options "suitable to a client's true needs." **Suitability** is a major buzzword in the industry and lax adherence to that standard tends to be the reason regulators pursue bank transgressions.

You won't always get far with that argument because banks are loathe to reverse financial transactions that have already settled, and they will insist that by signing the document your parent clearly understood the product and the associated risks. Nevertheless, the proceedings of numerous court cases and **arbitration** hearings show the elderly routinely are clueless about some financial product they bought or invested in, and have simply taken the word of the salesperson. And too often court documents reveal that those salespeople have misrepresented the truth, omitted key facts, or at worst flat-out lied to make the sale.

In a situation where the facts are egregious and you are appalled by a product the bank sold to your parents, consider legal action if that bank refuses to honor your demands that a transaction be reversed or nullified. Look for local elder law attorneys who specialize in cases in which the elderly have been victimized.

TIP: Encourage your parents to consult you before agreeing to stick money in anything other than a basic bank account. This applies not just to the banks they deal with, but also to any financial services institution that pitches a product to Mom or Dad. And before you give your approval, dissect that account to understand how it works. Call the sales agent and ask why your parent needs this product. Ask the person to describe the benefits and drawbacks of ownership, whether your parent can reclaim the money penalty-free whenever the money is needed, and how much commission will be earned on the sale—and remember never to accept "nothing" as the answer. If you don't feel equipped to make a yes/no decision, contact a trusted advisor, such as an attorney, to look over the documents and explain to you the ramifications of sticking money in this product. At the end of it all, if you still feel uncomfortable or if you simply cannot understand the rationale for putting money in this product, just say no.

Is the Money Working Hard Enough?

At the time this book was written, summer 2010, the average one-year certificate of deposit offered a yield of just 1.75%, while the average money market account paid less than 1%, according to Bankrate.com, a much-watched provider to interest rate data. That was just a pittance, and savvy savers could improve on it substantially by transferring money to online banks or opening accounts at local credit unions. The point here is that no matter the time period when you read these words, you will likely be able to find higher interest rates than your parent is currently earning, which, in turn, can help ease Mom/Dad's financial situation by improving their income.

As you examine the various bank accounts your parents own, make note of the interest rate the bank is paying on each account. And then spend some time looking for better yields.

Online banks such as EmigrantDirect.com, INGdirect. com, and others typically beat the rates offered by the local branches of big national and regional banks. Local credit unions are often an even better option. At the time of this writing, some credit unions were offering checking accounts paying 5%. Those accounts required certain conditions be met, including a requirement that some form of paycheck be directly deposited or a routine payment be automatically deducted, and that the account holder use a debit card ten or twelve times a month. But those necessities aren't that onerous when you think about it. You can have a parent's Social Security check directly deposited by the government, or you might have an insurance premium directly debited from the account.

As for the debit card requirement, parents can learn to use the debit card to buy gas, groceries, and pharmacy needs each month and likely meet the minimum usage. If necessary, have the bank emboss a card that you can use on behalf of your parents, if, for instance, you do their shopping. The benefits can be meaningful. Consider a $30,000 interest-bearing checking account: Earning just 0.58% (the national average in early 2010), that account earns $174 a year, or $14.50 a month. But move the money to a local credit union paying 5%, and now the account earns $1,500 a year, or $125 a month.

Clearly, that's a substantial bump in income, and can help a parent living on a fixed income improve or maintain a lifestyle. For that reason, look to consolidate multiple bank accounts into a single checking account that offers the greatest interest income. Most credit unions limit to between $10,000 and $30,000 the balance on which they offer the plumper yields. Keep the account as near that level as possible to maximize interest income, and put any additional cash into money market accounts of CDs that offer the highest yield (more to come in the next chapter on strategies for generating income from CDs).

TIP: If while monitoring your parent's checking account you routinely see bounced checks or overdraft charges, that's a clear sign Mom/Dad is having trouble paying bills on time, either because of inadequate cash flow, poor money management skills, or mental decline. To prevent the fees and fines from continuing to dun the account, contact the creditors (landlord/mortgage company, utility company, credit card provider, etc.) and arrange to have the bills sent to your house instead so that you can be sure the obligations are met on time. The money will still come from their accounts, unless the account balance isn't large enough to accommodate the expense—but that's an entirely different matter we'll deal with later in this chapter and the next chapter.

Alert your parents to this new arrangement and explain that you're trying to help them avoid the costly fees that are consuming money they could be allocating to other wants or needs.

The Safe-Deposit Box: What's in It
... and What Shouldn't Be

Just about everyone who has a safe-deposit box at the local bank uses it as a catchall for anything and everything that seems of potential value or possible importance. In the case of elderly parents, some of the items and documents stuffed into the box are old and useless, some are of unexpected value, and some should not be there. These items should, instead, be stored at home where you or your parents can call upon them quickly in an emergency.

This underscores an important point: It's crucial to make sure that documents are kept in the correct place. Even if you do have legal rights to a safe-deposit box, that means nothing at night or on a holiday or weekend when banks are closed. You could end up spending many stressful hours or days in an emergency waiting to gain access to the box so that you can obtain the document you need.

As a general rule, documents you don't have reason to reference often or that you're not likely to need in an emergency are best kept in a safe-deposit box. Many of these can be replaced if they're lost. Conversely, documents that you will quickly need to access if something happens to a parent are best kept in a fireproof lockbox at your home; make copies of those documents that your parents can keep in a similar lockbox at their house. Though many of these can also be replaced if lost, in an emergency you don't want the added stress of ginning up a duplicate copy, which can take hours or, more likely, days.

Documents best suited for a safe-deposit box:

- Original birth and death certificates, though keep a copy on hand at home in case you need to reference it for some reason.
- Marriage certificates.
- Divorce decrees.
- Baptismal records.
- Property deeds.
- Automobile titles.
- Stock and bond certificates.
- Home improvement records. You will need these to document the **cost basis** of your parent's home, which could factor into inheritance issues. If Mom/Dad gives you or other heirs the house before death, then the recipient will receive that home at its original cost basis. The home improvement records will help offset the overall profit on which the IRS will impose taxes. If the recipient picks up the house after a parent dies, the cost basis generally is the value of the home on the day of death. The records, in this case, won't matter, though any improvements you make going forward will matter, so keep those. And unlike the other papers listed here, these documents are usually expense receipts and they exist in only one place; they can't be replaced, so you need to protect them.

Documents best suited for a fireproof lockbox at home:

- Wills
- Trusts
- Power of attorney
- Medical power of attorney
- Annuity contracts
- Health insurance, burial insurance, and life insurance policies. You could keep these policies, as well as any annuity contracts, in a safe-deposit box. At the very least, though, keep in the lockbox the copy of the declarations page from each contract. This page, also called the "dec," details the policy number, the name on the policy, the name of the insurer and the insurer's phone number, the policy's coverage, and the insured's identifying information, which is often a Social Security number. Insurers generally don't require the policy itself to pay on the contract, but they will need all the identifying data, so it's best to have that handy in the event that accessing the safe-deposit box is inconvenient or impossible at a given moment.

TIP: You might be tempted to scan all these documents and store them on your personal computer, making them instantly available. This is not a good idea, though. Computers can be hacked or stolen, and all your parent's vital records can be used to cause financial havoc for them or for you. More important, many of these documents cannot be printed out and used when the need arises. You must have the original. For instance, birth certificates, auto titles, and other documents generally have raised seals that courts, government agencies, and others will insist on. The only useful purpose scanning serves is that it can make replacing a lost or destroyed original document substantially easier, since your scanned copy will have all the relevant information on it.

Income

THE CONCERN FOR MOST SENIORS is making sure they secure enough income on which to live and knowing the money they have will last until their last breath. No one wants to run out of money before running out of life. Helping parents manage their income, generate more income, and assure that the money keeps flowing for as long as they keep breathing is one of the key tasks you face in looking after Mom/Dad's finances.

This concept of "income" is not only the monthly checks that Social Security or a former employer sends to your parents each month. You have to look at this holistically. Several pages back I mentioned that you should make a parent's bank account work as hard as possible by seeking out online accounts or those offered by credit unions that sport the beefiest yields. That's one step in a process that includes determining when to begin taking Social Security payments (though many parents have probably already done that), how to think about structuring whatever investment portfolio Mom/Dad has, and how to build in permanent income by way of an **immediate annuity**.

The goal here is to generate as much monthly cash flow, after taxes, as possible from whatever sources exist for your parent—and to do so in a highly conservative fashion. You never want to put a parent in a situation where a risky investment goes sour and the income stream Mom/Dad depends on shrinks or, worse, evaporates. You want to provide for them rock-solid assurances that a basic level of income will always arrive. And if there are assets left over to employ, only then should you try to slightly tweak a portfolio for a modicum of additional growth.

Let's start with Social Security, since it is clearly the largest component of the average retiree's income.

When to Take Social Security

In most cases, the question of when to begin drawing on Social Security benefits is a nonissue because by the time you're called in to help your parents manage their finances, they're already well into their retirement and likely have been receiving Social Security checks for many years. If that's your parent's situation, then skip to the next section (unless you want to do a little prep work for your own retirement one day).

However, if Social Security checks aren't yet arriving, then continue reading. Social Security was never designed to provide retirees the same living standards they were accustomed to while working, nor are the monthly government checks supposed to be a retiree's only source of income—though I do realize that for many people Social Security is often the only source of meaningful income.

Generally speaking, Social Security aims to replace about 40% of the average worker's income, with the remainder of the necessary funds coming from savings and investments accumulated through a working career.

The most salient question about Social Security is when to begin receiving checks from the government. The Social Security Administration allows recipients to choose to apply for benefits anytime between the ages of sixty-two and seventy. In practical terms, that means three options are available:

- Take the money early, meaning between sixty-two and normal retirement age (see chart on page 80).
- Take the money at normal retirement age.
- Take the money late, meaning between normal retirement age and seventy.

Each option has its pros and cons. Before diving into this, though, know that like so many choices in life and retirement, there really is no one-size-fits-all answer because every retiree's circumstances are unique. Nevertheless, you do have to make a choice, and maximizing Social Security income for a parent (or, ultimately, yourself) hinges on having an adequate understanding of the options.

Note: If you're wondering about "normal retirement age," this chart shows you how it breaks down. Normal retirement age is 65 for birth years prior to 1943.

Year of Birth	Normal Retirement Age
1943–1954	66
1955	66 and 2 months
1956	66 and 4 months
1957	66 and 6 months
1958	66 and 8 months
1959	66 and 10 months
1960 and later	67

One set of facts is applicable to everyone: Take Social Security before your normal retirement age and your monthly income will be cut by as much as 30%. Wait until after your normal retirement age and monthly income can be 30% or more greater than the checks that would have arrived at normal retirement age. These decreases or increases are *permanent*, so once the drawdown begins, that's the base from which all future cost-of-living adjustments happen.

I want to say that again for emphasis: The increases or decreases in income are *permanent*. Mom/Dad can use that knowledge advantageously, because it means by waiting even a few years, the initial checks will be larger, which means all future cost-of-living adjustments will happen off that larger base, which ultimately means that later in life when medical costs ratchet higher your parents will be receiving larger Social Security checks from the government.

Alas, at the time of this writing roughly three-quarters of all Social Security recipients claimed their benefits early according to Social Security data. The rationale for doing so ranges from "I might not live long enough to receive any payments if I wait" to "it's my money and I want it now" to financial advisor recommendations to take Social Security early, even if a retiree doesn't need the cash to live on, because the retiree can, in theory, invest the money and earn a better return than can the government.

Some of that is understandable, but the logic is generally shortsighted. Most retirees do far better financially by waiting at least until normal retirement age—and a savvier strategy often is to wait slightly longer. And the whole notion of "doing better on your own" was sorely tested—and it widely failed—in the economic collapse of 2008 and early 2009.

Consider a few statistics from the Society of Actuaries, the mathematicians paid to calculate risk and uncertainty, generally for insurance companies and the like. First off, 67% of retirees underestimate by five or more years their life expectancy after they've reached retirement age. The bulk of them (about 60%) expect they'll only make it to eighty at best. Yet once you've reached sixty-five years old, life expectancy is another sixteen years for a man and nineteen years for a woman. And if you reach a life expectancy of eighty-three as a man, then your life expectancy at that point jumps to ninety. What's more, reaching sixty-five as a couple means there's a 40% chance that one partner will live to see ninety-five.

The various researchers who have examined the question

of when to begin drawing on Social Security have routinely come away suggesting that the best approach is one of patience. A study out of the Center for Retirement Research at Boston College, just to pick one example, determined that any retiree who expects to live until at least eighty (and most do harbor such expectations) would do much better to delay taking benefits until sixty-six instead of taking them at sixty-two. (The math changes over time, since the Social Security Administration is slowly pushing full retirement age to sixty-seven. But for parents who are about to retire or who are already retired—and haven't started taking Social Security—the numbers hold.)

Effectively, the decision boils down to this:

- Take Social Security early and face the risk of living a long time in retirement on what is a self-imposed, decreased income stream.
- Or show some patience by filing for Social Security later and, ultimately, live on a greater sum of money that will grow even larger over time—though you have to find a way to fund those early years between the time Social Security eligibility begins and when payments finally start.

Remember: Social Security is a lifelong payout. So holding off even just a couple of years can make a meaningful difference in retirement income later in life, thanks to the cumulative nature of those cost-of-living inflation adjustments. See the chart on the next page:

			Age Attained			
		65	**70**	**75**	**80**	**85**
Retirement Age	**62**	$750.00	$819.55	$950.08	$1,101.40	$1,276.82	$1,480.19
	65	$1,000.00	$1,092.73	$1,266.77	$1,468.53	$1,702.43	$1,973.59
	70	$1,320.00		$1,672.14	$1,938.46	$2,247.21	$2,605.13

The key numbers in the chart are the dollar values under the "Age Attained" heading. They represent the monthly Social Security check after various periods in retirement for a retiree who claims Social Security early (sixty-two), at retirement age (sixty-five), and later in retirement (seventy). They're all based on annual cost-of-living adjustments averaging 3% annually, though that could be higher or lower at any given point going forward. A retiree who is eligible for $1,000 a month at age sixty-five who opts to claim Social Security early will see benefits reduced to $750 a month (this is based on Social Security data that may be somewhat different when you read these words, but the overarching concept is the same). Waiting until seventy jacks up the payout to $1,320 a month.

But look at how those dollar differences escalate as cost-of-living adjustments kick in through the years. Notice first the numbers highlighted in gray; they don't match the corresponding $1,000 and $1,320 figures that were supposed to mark the income levels for waiting until sixty-five or seventy. Here's why: The retiree who chooses to take Social Security at sixty-two is looking at dollar values as of that date. In other words, Social Security provides the sixty-two-year-old with a document that says based on today the monthly income is $750 at sixty-two, $1,000 at sixty-five, and $1,320 at seventy. Yet by sixty-five, three more years of inflation adjustment have taken place so at that point the $1,000 has grown to nearly $1,093. For the retiree who waits until seventy, we're now talking about eight years of inflation adjustments and a paycheck worth more than $1,672 instead of $1,320.

By age eighty, the retiree who waited the longest (that is, until age seventy) is pulling in nearly $1,000 more every month. That larger sum is arriving just about the time health care costs are likely rising, making it easier to afford the outlays. Heck, just waiting from sixty-two to seventy is the equivalent of earning an annual return of 10.5%, healthy by any investment standards—and undermines the financial advisor spiel that a retiree taking Social Security early can invest the money and earn better returns. Over the history of the **S&P 500 stock index**, returns have averaged right at 10%, but Social Security doesn't run the risk of blowing apart in a financial crisis like stocks and bonds do.

Look what happens if you just wait three years, until age sixty-five: You pull in $1,093 a month instead of the cost-of-living adjusted $819 you would otherwise receive had you opted to take Social Security at age sixty-two. That's a 33% difference and the same as having earned about 10% a year just for waiting it out a little longer.

You might rightly be thinking, "But what about all the money my parents are forsaking by waiting?" And that's a good point. After all, a parent who claims the $750 a month at sixty-two will have taken in nearly $28,000 by age sixty-five. For a parent who waits, that's $28,000 that has to be replaced somehow in order to afford life.

And I'm going to get to that in just a few pages. But first: You can't look at Social Security as a one-time event. It's a choice for the rest of a lifetime. And you need to understand the true financial impact of taking the payments earlier or later, factoring in the higher inflation-adjusted payments received by waiting. Before making any decision on when to claim Social Security, calculate the "breakeven period." In plain speak, the breakeven is an age; it's the age at which the total benefits received from taking Social Security later in life surpass the amount of money you would have received if you'd opted to take Social Security early. Here's another chart to consider—a graphic way of looking at the break-even period, again using a sixty-two-year-old parent who claims $750 a month instead of waiting for age sixty-five and that $1,000 monthly payment they would receive (and, remember, that $1,000 a sixty-two-year-old would receive three years later at sixty-five benefits from the 3% annual cost-of-living adjustment, so the beginning monthly payments at sixty-five are actually $1,093):

Age	Annual Benefits (start age 62)	Cumulative Benefits	Annual Benefits (start age 66)	Cumulative Benefits
62	$9,000	$9,000		
63	$9,270	$18,270		
64	$9,548	$27,818		
65	$9,835	$37,653	$13,113	$13,113
66	$10,130	$47,782	$13,506	$26,619
67	$10,433	$58,216	$13,911	$40,530
68	$10,746	$68,962	$14,329	$54,859
69	$11,069	$80,031	$14,758	$69,617
70	$11,401	$91,432	$15,201	$84,818
72	$11,743	$103,175	$15,657	$100,476
72	$12,095	$115,270	$16,127	$116,603
73	$12,458	$127,728	$16,611	$133,214
75	$12,832	$140,560	$17,109	$150,323
75	$13,217	$153,777	$17,622	$167,945
76	$13,613	$167,390	$18,151	$186,096
77	$14,022	$181,412	$18,696	$204,792
78	$14,442	$195,854	$19,256	$224,048
79	$14,876	$210,730	$19,834	$243,882
80	$15,322	$226,052	$20,429	$264,312
81	$15,782	$241,833	$21,042	$285,354
82	$16,255	$258,088	$21,673	$307,027
83	$16,743	$274,831	$22,324	$329,351
84	$17,245	$292,076	$22,993	$352,344
85	$17,762	$309,838	$23,683	$376,027

The key numbers are again shaded in gray. At age seventy-two, the cumulative benefits received for a retiree claiming benefits at sixty-five surpass the cumulative benefits had that same retiree started taking Social Security at sixty-two. That means the break-even period for waiting is just six years (sixty-five to seventy-two). You can search online for "Social Security break-even calculator" and find a few that will help you crunch the numbers specific to your parent's situation.

If you talk to financial planners, as I noted several paragraphs back, you're likely to hear that it's smarter to take Social Security early and allow tax deferred accounts like an IRA or a 401(k) plan to grow undisturbed for as long as possible. That gives a retiree income to live on now from Social Security, and then a bump in income later when the IRA starts flooding out.

Sounds logical. But not so fast: A 2009 study by insurance giant Prudential shreds that bit of conventional wisdom. Prudential found that such a strategy actually does more harm than good when it comes to maximizing retirement income, which is the goal of just about every retiree I've ever met or interviewed.

Instead Prudential found that a strategy of *drawing on an IRA first* and waiting to take Social Security later actually creates a larger pot of after-tax income—and that's the most important income because it is truly spendable income.

The issue that Prudential highlights, and that many advisors and planners routinely overlook or don't understand, is the taxation of Social Security and non–Social Security income. There's no reason to bog down this book with a bunch of tax facts, but the bottom line is that Social Security income is not taxed like IRA income—and that has a massive impact on total retirement income over time.

Every dollar that Mom/Dad pulls out of an IRA, a pension, a 401(k), etc. is taxed at **ordinary income rates**— generally the highest rates. That means every single dollar (except those coming from a Roth IRA) is taxed at the highest possible rate for your parent's income bracket.

This is not so with Social Security income. Social Security is generally not taxable income until a taxpayer's total income reaches a certain level. Once combined income— meaning Social Security plus all other income for an individual retiree—reaches a certain threshold, up to 50% of Social Security benefits are taxed. At a second threshold, the highest threshold, up to 85% of benefits are taxed.

Those thresholds move around, but as of 2010 they were:

Tax Rates				
	1st threshold	SS tax rate	2nd threshold	SS tax rate
Single person	$25,000	50%	$34,000	85%
Married filing jointly	$32,000	50%	$44,000	85%

Combine this tax advantage with the longevity insurance built into Social Security (the fact that checks keep arriving until death and that they contain a cost-of-living adjustment) and what you find is that Social Security is a far better source of income than financial planners would have you believe— or that they often even realize themselves.

What It Means in Real Life

The benefit of this tax treatment is that it lowers the amount of taxes Mom/Dad will have to pay on Social Security, providing for greater spendable income and the ability to stretch a nest egg further.

Here's what I mean by lower taxes. This chart is courtesy of Prudential:

Social Security Taxes					
How combined IRA income and Social Security income is taxed:			How every dollar of "delayed" Social Security income is taxed		
IRA income		$1	Social Security Income		$1
Tax rate	x	25%	Combined income formula	x	50%
IRA tax (A)	=	0.25	Amount of S.S. taxable income	=	0.5
Additional S.S. subject to tax		$1	% of S.S. income subject to taxes	x	85%
% of S.S. income subject to taxes	x	85%			
Taxable S.S. income	=	0.85	Taxable S.S. income	=	0.425
Tax rate	x	25%	Tax rate	x	25%
S.S. tax (B)	=	0.2125	S.S. tax	=	0.1062
Total tax in cents (A+B)	=	0.4645	Total tax in cents	=	0.1062
Total tax in percentage	or	46.25%	Total tax in percentage	or	10.62%

This chart effectively shows that every dollar of income from an IRA, 401(k) plan, or such that Mom/Dad bring in can have a dramatic impact on the taxation of Social Security dollars. (By the way, in a situation where only 50% of Social Security is taxed, the comparable tax rates—those listed as "total tax in percentage"—are 37.5% and 6.25%.)

So what is this saying, you might be wondering. It's saying that to the degree possible Mom/Dad is better off taking as many IRA dollars as possible early on and as few Social Security dollars as possible.

I want to go through an example with you to show this in action. But first you have to know that there are three tests to determine the level at which Social Security is taxed. I know this is mind-numbing minutiae, but it really does have the power to help your parents live more comfortably, and that will mean less stress on you. The combined income formula I mentioned a few pages back taxes Social Security based on the smallest of:

- **Test 1**: 85% of the total benefits; or

- **Test 2**: 50% of the benefits plus 85% of any excess over the second threshold; or

- **Test 3**: 50% of the excess over the first threshold, plus 35% of the excess over the second threshold.

OK, so here's what it all looks like in practical terms. Again, this is from Prudential. The chart on the next page represents the huge drop in **adjusted gross income (AGI)** for a retiree who waits until seventy to begin taking Social Security. A drop in AGI does not imply a drop in income; as you will see, total income remains the same. AGI is simply the amount of income, after adjustments, on which taxes are due.

But because taxable income declines so significantly, total taxes due will decline, meaning more money for Mom/Dad to live on.

Tax Impact of Delaying Social Security Payments
(married couple filing jointly)

Approach A: Taking reduced Social Security early and supplementing with IRA withdrawals
Approach B: Delaying Social Security

			APPROACH A	APPROACH B
	IRA income		$45,000	$20,000
	Social Security income	+	$45,000	$70,000
	Total pre-tax income	=	**$90,000**	**$90,000**
	Adjusted Gross Income		$45,000	$20,000
	Tax exempt income	+	$0	$0
	Modified AGI	=	**$45,000**	**$20,000**
	Social Security benefits		$45,000	$70,000
TEST 1	85% of Social Security benefits **(Total Test 1)**		**$38,250**	**$59,250**
	A) 50% of Social Security benefits		$22,500	$35,000
	B) Combined Income (AGI + A)		$67,500	$55,000
	C) Less second threshold		$44,000	$44,000
TEST 2	D) Excess above second threshold (B-C)		$23,500	$11,000
	E) 85% of excess (D x 85%)		$19,975	$9,350
	Total Test s (A + E)		**$42,475**	**$44,350**
	B) Combined Income (AGI + A above)		$67,500	$55,000
	F) Less first threshold		$32,000	$32,000
	G) Excess above first threshold (B-F)		$35,500	$23,000
TEST 3	H) 50% of excess above first threshold (G x 50%)		$17,750	$11,500
	I) 35% of excess over second threshold (D x 35%)		$8,225	$3,850
	Total Test 3 (H + I)		**$25,975**	**$15,350**
	Amount includable in gross income (least of the three tests)		$25,975	$15,350
	Taxable income (Modified AGI + lowest test)		**$70,975**	**$35,350**
	Difference between Approach A and Approach B			-$35,625
	Percentage of income removed from AGI by trading IRA income for Social Security income			142.5%
	% drop in AGI caused by switch of IRA income to Social Security income			50.2%

The key difference here: By delaying Social Security and drawing on an IRA or a 401(k) first, Mom/Dad are allowing their ultimate Social Security check to grow dramatically, meaning that when your parent does begins to draw on Social Security, they will not have to draw as much from an IRA or 401(k) later. Along with the higher Social Security payments later in life, this strategy will allow Mom/Dad to stretch a nest egg further.

The Cost of Waiting

You're probably thinking: Wait. If Mom/Dad doesn't take Social Security until seventy, then they're going to deplete their IRA/401(k) more quickly in the early years, before the government checks start arriving, leaving a much smaller nest egg to live on.

In the early years, that's true. The IRA drawdown is larger than it would be if Mom/Dad signed up to receive Social Security when first eligible.

But once the Social Security kicks in at a higher level, the IRA doesn't have to work nearly as hard. The drawdowns fall precipitously, well below those for a retiree who took Social Security earlier. After several years, the cumulative IRA withdrawals for the retiree taking Social Security early exceed the cumulative IRA withdrawals for the retiree waiting to take Social Security later—and the gap grows wider and wider with each year. That, as you might recognize, has huge implications on the longevity of your parent's nest egg.

By reducing the withdrawal rate longer term, you're helping your parents stretch their retirement savings over a greater number of years.

By waiting to take Social Security until later in retirement, total Social Security payments are larger, while cumulative IRA withdrawals and taxes are markedly lower.

The obvious message is that retirees who withdraw from an IRA first and then claim Social Security benefits later reduce their tax burden. Do it the other way around—take Social Security first and supplement that with IRA withdrawals later—and the tax burden is higher, as is the longer-term burden on the IRA itself.

401(k) and IRA Distributions:
At Some Point They're *Mandatory*

If your parents have either a 401(k) retirement savings plan or an individual retirement account (aside from a Roth IRA, but more on that in a moment), and they are not yet pulling money from those accounts, they will come to an age where Internal Revenue Service regulations require that withdrawals begin—or else.

That age is seventy and six months. And the "or else" is, as usual with the IRS, a penalty.

By April 1 of the year after a retiree turns seventy and a half, money must begin coming out of an IRA, what's known as the **required minimum distribution**. (There is a loophole: If a parent is still working *full time and does not own more than 5% of the business*, the required minimum distribution doesn't apply.) Mom or Dad's age and the value of the account determine the amount of money that must come out. The IRS uses the "Uniform Lifetime Table" to determine that sum. Here's how it worked in tax year 2009:

Let's assume your parent has $75,000 in an IRA and must begin taking the required distributions at seventy-one (remember, it's April 1 of the year *after* reaching seventy and a half). The **Uniform Lifetime Table** for 2009 indicates a distribution period of 26.5 years. So, you just divide the $75,000 account balance by the distribution period and you get $2,830—the amount of money that must be withdrawn that year from the IRA. The following year, a different distribution period will be used to determine the required minimum withdrawal. By the way, this example assumes a single parent for the sake of simplicity.

If both spouses are still alive and one is the sole beneficiary of the IRA *and* is more than ten years younger than the IRA owner, then the distribution period is based on the IRS's Joint Life and Last Survivor Expectancy Table. The various tables and rules are found at the IRS's website, www.irs.gov. Search for Publication 590 if you want to root through the details or determine the distribution period for the current year. With a little time and attention, you can figure this out on your own. Then again, you might want a professional tax preparer to ensure the returns follow the rules accurately if you'd rather not muck around with the tedium.

The big caveat with required minimum distribution comes with a **Roth IRA**. It imposes no minimum distributions. A retiree who lives to even one hundred or beyond can keep a Roth and never have to touch it. That can make a Roth an effective tool for estate planning. A Roth IRA allows parents to leave to their heirs a potentially large sum of money that escapes income taxes, though not necessarily estate taxes (for more on Roth IRAs, see pages 147–48).

If parents have a traditional IRA and determine they will not likely tap into it for their retirement living needs, then you, your parents, and a financial planner should discuss the possibility of converting that account into a Roth IRA because of the potential tax advantage to you or the heir set to receive the account balance.

When a nonspouse beneficiary (let's assume this is you for the sake of simplicity) receives a Roth IRA in an inheritance, you must take complete distribution of the money, either by December 31 of the fifth year following the original owner's death, or over your natural life.

If you chose the first option, you can effectively let the value of the Roth grow for five years and then take a lump-sum payout of cash tax free to bring the balance to $0. Or, if you chose the second option, you must begin taking tax-free withdrawals, again by December 31 of the year after the original owner died.

The potential problem to keep in mind is that Roths require that the account be in place for at least five years before any withdrawal is made, otherwise taxes are imposed. With the first distribution option, since you wait five years before touching the money, you can easily satisfy that rule and claim all the cash tax-free. With the second option, that might not be the case. If the Roth isn't five years old by the time your parent dies and you begin taking distributions, you could owe taxes on the profits and earnings, though never on the original principal, since taxes on that money were paid before the cash went into the account.

One last note: As with requirements that retirees take required minimum distribution by age seventy and a half, failure to take distribution of an inherited IRA according to the rules could subject you or the heir to a penalty equal to 50% of the account balance. That's a steep price to pay for what otherwise is money the government can't touch. So pay very close attention if you ultimately inherit a Roth IRA.

How Much Income Does a Parent Need?

Obviously, there's no single answer to that question. It's all about the facts and circumstances unique to your parent's financial needs and wants. Age and mobility also play a huge role here. Younger, active retirees typically consume more money because they're out enjoying the freedom they've earned after decades of work. As parents grow older and begin to slow down, though, spending patterns often change and slow down as well—and then ramp up again when the end of life is approaching and the costs of nursing homes, assisted living centers, and/or home health aides arise.

Whatever the case, this question of how much money a parent needs to live on in retirement is a matter of much debate between financial advisors. Some calculate that a retiree needs only about 70% of preretirement income to live a similar lifestyle in retirement, since so many costs go away, like commuting expenses, work clothes, lunchtime meals bought away from the office, educational and other expenses for children, and a mortgage (if it has been paid in full). Others, including many retirees, peg the number closer to 100%, noting that workaday expenses are simply traded for other costs like increased health care and prescription expenses. Also, with all the refinancing and moving from one house to another that Americans do, many retirees still pay a mortgage late in life. And if you listen to people who have been retired for several years, they will often report that their costs typically rise in the early years of retirement as they travel on holiday to visit children and relatives, pick up new hobbies, and spend more time eating out.

Ultimately, how much income Mom and Dad need is a function of the life they're living at the stage of retirement in which they ask you to get involved. You might find your parent is living a little too well, consuming money at a pace that threatens to deplete a nest egg too quickly. Or, possibly, parents are living so far below their means that quality of life suffers. When called upon by parents, your duty is to assess the situation, and then help determine how best to deploy the cash flow coming in and, where possible, how to increase a parent's income.

Begin by helping parents build a budget. You might call this a "wants-and-needs budget" since this budget's aim is to separate the needs that must be funded from the wants that might be funded only if extra income exists each month. In practical terms this is what *every* budget seeks to accomplish, even for those who are much younger. But defining needs and wants is particularly crucial for retirees on a fixed income because their peace of mind often comes in knowing with absolute certainty that they have enough money coming in each month to cover their basic costs of living—housing, food, insurance, utilities, prescriptions, and such.

Though people occasionally dread constructing a budget, it's really quite painless. More important, it provides a certain degree of financial power and the security that comes in knowing you have enough money to cover the costs of your life. The power, meanwhile, comes because when you know where your money is going, you have the opportunity to re-direct those funds to what you determine are more impor-tant expense categories. Here's what I mean, as it relates to parents: My mom asked me to help her manage her money, so I had her e-mail a memo to me that detailed her finances— all the money coming in, all the mandatory expenses she had to pay, and the amount of credit card debt she had. I spent a week or so going through all the numbers, cutting subscrip-tions here and there, and doing all I could to stretch her lim-ited income across her life.

Then, over Sunday brunch at a local restaurant, I laid out the details for her. But it wasn't me dictating what she could and couldn't spend. I showed her where her spending stood at that moment, and how it would change based on my sugges-tions. But I let her make the decisions about what she would and wouldn't cut. I gave her a menu of her discretionary ex-penses and let her pick which ones were the most important and which ones she didn't mind losing. The only caveat: The combined costs of the ones she kept had to be less than the amount of her discretionary income.

That's what wants-and-needs budgeting is all about— small line-item decisions that give you and your parent the knowledge necessary to make spending decisions that mean the most to Mom or Dad.

Through this process we will also get into ways of increas-ing income, where possible. But we'll start with the expense side of the ledger.

First things first: Build a profile of your parent's typical monthly expenses. (This will be an exercise that requires a decent block of time and effort, but it is necessary and will ultimately help you to better help a parent live more comfortably and securely.) In a notebook or, better still, a spreadsheet on your computer, label two columns: "needs" and "wants." Then go through credit card statements, the checkbook register, and old bank statements for the last six to twelve months and catalog the expenses as best you can into fundamental categories that fit under those two master headings. It will look something like the list on page 101, though the categories here are not exhaustive. The list you come up with will be unique to the spending patterns in your parent's life:

Needs like cable TV, Internet access, and mobile phones clearly might not be needs in many instances, but in other cases they very well might. Moreover, there are certain costs on the needs side that might no longer fit the needs category, depending on your parent's situation. If a parent has a car and all the associated costs with upkeep, yet rarely drives, a more cost-effective solution might be to sell the vehicle, earmark the savings for a bank account, and use some of that money to hire a cab when necessary. Better yet, maybe Mom/Dad can pay a friend or neighbor a little gas money to tote them to the supermarket, pharmacy, barber shop, etc. when those needs arise.

There's also a case to be made for cutting out life insurance premiums at some point. Though often misused, life insurance is designed as an income-replacement vehicle in the event a breadwinner dies. The payout aims to help a spouse afford a mortgage and the cost of living, to afford a retirement, or to help pay for the education of young children. By the time a retiree passes on, mortgages in many instances are already paid off and a child's education is many years past. The only real concern might be a spouse's ability to pay for the cost of living in retirement, though at this stage of the game other assets and income streams such as Social Security, pensions, and withdrawals from retirement savings accounts are available. Or the money earmarked for the life insurance premium might better be used to afford more important costs. Dropping life insurance coverage, thus, saves money. But facts and circumstances are different from one family to the next, so spend a little time with an independent financial planner to discuss this option. Do not, however, call the insurance agent who sold the policy and seek advice on this question. That's like asking a monkey to rate the taste of a banana; the answer you get will be exceedingly biased.

Pet care is a bit dicier. In practical terms, having a pet is really a want since a cat or dog is clearly not necessary for survival. But a beloved animal can bring companionship and give an elderly person a sense of feeling needed, both of which are powerfully strong emotions that can help maintain happiness. Similarly, some of the wants, such as restaurant meals, entertainment, or club dues, might really fit the needs category since they are about companionship and maintaining ties with friends later in life when those ties can be so important to mental and even physical well-being.

Another example from my experiences with my family helps to illustrate the challenge of balancing wants and needs. My grandmother lost my grandfather back in 1991 and has been alone ever since. When she finally retired (she worked into her eighties just because she wanted to stay busy) she began spending in a way that an outside observer might call irresponsible. She was taking friends to lunches and

NEEDS	*Wants*
Mortgage/rent	Travel
Homeowners/renters insurance	Subscriptions
Property taxes	Premium cable channels
Electric/gas utilities	Restaurant meals
Basic cable TV	Hobbies
Internet access	New car
Fixed-line telephone	Motor home
Mobile phone	Non-basic clothing
Groceries	Movies/entertainment
Prescriptions	Gifts for friends
Health insurance premiums	Club dues
Life insurance premiums	Non-basic groceries
Transportation	
Car payment	
Gasoline	
Maintenance	
Auto insurance premiums	
Debt payments	
Medical	
Home equity loan	
Credit cards	
Pet care	

brunches, and she was holding big backyard cookouts for a score or more of friends and neighbors.

The reality, though, was that her finances just weren't built for that. I could have stepped in and made my concern known; she relied on me to steer her finances. But I also knew what she lived through growing up as an orphan. I knew some of the challenges and difficulties she'd lived with through the years. And I saw the spending as her way of buying some of the happiness she felt she'd missed out on in her early years. So I kept my mouth shut. Having been raised by her, I knew my grandmother well enough to know she would rein herself in at some point because of her awareness of her money. She ultimately did. But I was ready to step in and stop the spending if she didn't.

Ultimately, all of these decisions are for you and your parent to make, based on their lifestyle.

Once you've compiled the list of wants and needs, tally the monthly costs for each category so that you have an annual figure, and then divide by twelve to get a monthly average. You want to see the average expense for the month as a whole, as well as the average monthly expense for each category. (This is where it's nice to have put this together on a spreadsheet, which will make easy work of the math.)

Now tally your parent's total income for each month. This will include Social Security and pension payments, as well as any other payment that might be routine, such as alimony, income from an annuity, dividend and interest income, and so on. Note: If a parent has a certificate of deposit for which the monthly interest payments accumulate inside the CD and are not distributed to a checking or savings account, do not include that in this income calculation. That is not money available for spending each month because doing so would require that the CD contract be broken, which would result in penalties and fees.

Ultimately, you can arrange for the interest instead to flow into a checking account if that cash flow would help your parent meet monthly spending needs; just restructure the way the CD pays out the next time it matures. If the CD matures several years down the road, but increased income is necessary now, then breaking the contract and taking the financial hit—usually about three months' worth of interest payments—likely makes sense since immediate income is more important.

Finally, match your parent's average monthly costs against monthly income. At this point, bring your parent into the process. This is where Mom/Dad take a look at what their life really costs relative to their monthly income. This is where a parent—with your help, if necessary—gets to determine which costs are really needs, which ones are really wants, and the best way of spreading the current level of income across all the expenses. Your ultimate aim is to show Mom/Dad the degree to which current income is able to cover fixed costs, or needs. Don't worry yet about wants.

If income exceeds expenses, the best situation, this exercise can help parents realize their finances are more secure than they or you might have imagined, or that they can afford a more comfortable lifestyle than they might be living. At the very least, they can see where they're spending on items that ultimately don't mean much and how they might redirect that money to expense categories that are more important.

The more challenging situation, and the one this exercise is really designed to address, arises when expenses exceed income. If that's the case with your parents, three choices exist: They must either cut spending, find strategies to increase their income, or you can step in to subsidize their monthly cash flow to cover some or all of the shortfall. This is another situation in which you might need help with starting the conversation, since parents don't want to feel like you are dictating to them what they can or cannot buy. So maybe try something similar to my approach when I was helping my mom with her budget in preparation for the Sunday brunch meeting.

CONVERSATION STARTER

"Mom/Dad, I've gone through your income and expenses and I have some suggestions I'd like to make. But I want you to know the final decision about how you want to spend your money is yours. I'm just going to give you the details and offer some options, and then help you make the decisions that best fit what you want."

TIP: If you elect to subsidize your parents, consider paying certain bills for them instead of giving cash. As with kids, cash given to a parent might be seen as "found money" rather than money to pay for necessities. As such, it could be wasted. Better to directly pay bills for utilities, insurance, health care premiums, etc. This way you know certain basics are paid for, and that leaves parents with their own cash to spend on discretionary wants.

When Mom/Dad is in a shortfall, do not allow your parent to float the difference each month on a credit card. Over time the balance will grow to a level that ultimately undermines Mom/Dad's entire financial structure, and at that point fixing the problems will be substantially more burdensome on you and draconian on them.

So, let's build a budget. This is how easy it can be:

Step 1: Cut all discretionary expenses, the wants. Ultimately your parents can build some wants back into their budget, but for the time being slice every want on the list.

Step 2: Compare fixed expenses to current income.

   A. If current income is greater than fixed expenses, skip to Step 3.

   B. If fixed expenses are greater than current income, look to find where expenses can be reduced. That might mean, for example, getting rid of or scaling back cable/satellite TV service, doing away with a mobile phone, or, if Mom/Dad still have a mortgage, refinancing a house if lower interest rates prevail. If you cannot cut fixed expenses enough to fall below the current level of income, you'll need to help your parent increase the amount of money flowing in each month. You can jump to the section labeled "Laddering CDs" in the next chapter, which is where the discussion begins on increasing income.

Step 3: Once fixed expenses are covered, and if there's money remaining in the budget, work with your parents to reinstitute some of the wants they can afford. This is where the power that I mentioned earlier in the chapter comes in. How your parent wants to spend discretionary money is entirely up to Mom/Dad. They can allocate all of it to restaurant meals and entertainment; they can direct it to hobbies or travel; they can stash some of it in a savings account for unexpected expenses (and you should encourage that). But once the discretionary income is accounted for in the budget, that's the end of it—no more spending.

What you've done is fit your parents' lifestyle into their existing means. At this point, consider locking in some degree of permanent income that will cover some or all of a parent's fixed costs until their death—and there's more on that in the next chapter. It will give both them and you some peace of mind to know that their basic needs will always be met.

Finding a Lost Pension

Your parents might have a pension they don't even know about.

Mom or Dad through the years might have changed jobs, and along the way lost contact with a previous employer. Or an employer might have terminated a pension plan years ago, and the company records transferred several times through merger and acquisition activity, and your parent could have simply forgotten a pension was even due, or that one ever even existed.

Whatever the case, the Pension Benefit Guaranty Corporation is a federal unit that backs the benefits provided by private sector pension plans. When those plans are terminated or wrapped up in bankruptcy proceedings, they end up in the hands of the PBGC, which is charged with making sure the money in the plans makes it to the rightful recipients.

The problem is that the PBGC isn't always able to find those recipients. Thousands of retirees are owed pensions ranging from a couple bucks to several hundred thousand dollars, though the average benefit is about $5,000.

The PBGC has established a website (search.pbgc. gov) where people can search free of charge for unclaimed pensions by last name or company name. The companies that have made it onto the database largely come from the airline, steel, transportation, machinery, retail, apparel, and financial services industries. And the states with the greatest number of people who have a missing pension at PBGC are New York, California, New Jersey, Pennsylvania, Texas, Florida, and Illinois.

If you find a parent's name on the list, you'll need to supply proof of identity. Once verified—and that can take more than a month—the benefits checks will arrive within two months for those who are already retired, or they'll begin arriving once the beneficiary reaches retirement age. If someone owed benefits has died, survivors in many cases are eligible to claim the pension.

4

The Money, Part 2

Making the Money Last

JUST ABOUT EVERYONE WHO helps manage Mom/Dad's money in retirement worries about one key question: Are my parents spending too much?

In some ways that concern presents a tricky balancing act: You've been called in because your parents want your assistance, but at the same time this is *their* money. They spent a working career earning it and saving it, and they should be able to spend it on whatever they want to feel happy or comfortable in retirement.

Of course if a parent's spending is carefree and you can see the overall balance shriveling at a quick pace, you do have reason to fret. After all, what happens if the well runs dry? Where do your parents turn for the money they need to live on? Do you step up and start covering their expenses? Do you let them live on Social Security alone, even though that might not cover anything more than the bare basics?

Those are the very questions one of my friends on the West Coast struggled with for a couple of years. She saw the spending was out of control, but she didn't have the voice to tell her parents to rein it in. She mentioned her worry, but Mom shot her down with a "Don't worry about it, Honey. Dad and I are fine."

Only they weren't.

And my friend, feeling put-upon and exceedingly frustrated and angry, had to step in and become her parent's personal ATM. She ultimately forced them to downscale their home so that they could capture some of the equity and use that to supplement their Social Security. But the episode was painful and caused great friction that my friend says, "I'm not sure my parents ever really got over."

Before that happens to you—or if you see it coming—your quest is to help your parents stretch their dollars as far as possible, and help them generate the most income they can from the assets they own.

How Much Money Should Mom/Dad Withdraw from a Nest Egg?

HERE'S THE DILEMMA MANY retirees struggle with: They quit working and find that they suddenly have a large sum of cash, either from a 401(k) plan or a lump-sum pension payment or, maybe, a deferred compensation plan.

When you're accustomed to living on a certain amount of income a year and now have access to an account that is often multiples larger than the salary you earned in your best year, you reflexively perceive that you are wealthier than you are and, thus, you spend more freely.

The missing link that retirees don't always recognize is just how long this money must last. Think about it this way: If you earned $75,000 a year, but you have a $1 million retirement account, you think you have all the money you're ever going to need. But if you withdrew $75,000 a year to live on (equal to 7.5% of the original nest egg), your account would be approaching empty in about twelve or fifteen years, depending on the investment returns the account earns and the rate of inflation in the overall economy. If you retired at sixty-five, that would mean the nest egg is gone by eighty or so—yet these days most eighty-year-olds are still quite active and full of life.

What do you do at that point when you're still alive and your million-dollar cushion is gone?

What we're talking about here is something the financial services community increasingly refers to as "decumulation," effectively reverse accumulation (i.e., spending what you've saved). Throughout a working career you accumulate assets; in retirement you decumulate those same assets, spending them as you go along. Sounds simple enough, spending money, but decumulation can be a perilous venture because the pot of cash is limited and the factors involved are all unknowable. The financial community has spent the past decade trying to come up with "the number," the amount of money a retiree likely needs to accumulate prior to retiring in order to afford life after work. The reality, though, is that no such number exists because it can't in any legitimate form. No one has any clue how long they'll live in retirement, how their health will hold out, and how much they'll have to spend on doctors and medicines. Nor can they predict the rate at which inflation will grow during those years in retirement, or what size returns the financial markets will generate prior to retirement and after. All those factors play leading roles in how long a nest egg lasts.

The key question every retiree needs to ask, then, isn't how big a nest egg do I need but, rather, how much can I spend each year and feel relatively assured that the assets I have accumulated will last? That's the answer you have to help Mom and Dad determine so that they feel secure during their retirement—and so that you feel secure during their retirement, too.

The key to helping parents avoid depleting a nest egg too quickly is working with them on strategies to determine a realistic withdrawal rate, or how much money they can pull from the total asset base each year and feel relatively certain that no matter the direction of the economy or the investment markets, their overall portfolio will continue to generate sufficient income for a sufficiently long period of time—namely for as long as they live. If this is not something you feel comfortable doing yourself—and don't feel bad if you don't since not everyone is at ease with big financial decisions—find a fee-only financial planner and buy your parents a few hours of planning advice.

TIP: Find fee-only planners in your local area through the Financial Planning Association (www.fpanet.org) or the National Association of Personal Financial Advisors (www.napfa.org). Because the planners charge either a set fee or an hourly fee, they will not try to steer you or Mom/Dad into a particular product. As such, they are generally not beholden to a potentially dodgy financial services company or squirrelly products that do more to line the seller's pocket than your parent's nest egg.

If you care to step in and try to help your parents on your own, or if you just want some knowledge you can use when chatting with the advisor, then here's what you need to understand when it comes to figuring out how much money Mom or Dad should spend from their account.

Recognize from the outset that what you are trying to do is create for your parents a paycheck in retirement that will supplement whatever Social Security pays. You don't save and invest over the years in preparation for retirement so that you can drain the assets willy-nilly. You accumulate a nest egg to gradually disburse money throughout retirement to help afford life when a paycheck from an employer stops. In essence, retirees pay themselves a salary from the only pot of funding that's available.

As parents drain some of their assets each year, the remainder of the portfolio aims to grow a little bit to replace some, maybe even all of the money withdrawn. Pulling out too much money puts an undue burden on the rest of the account, and generally speaking the rest of the account isn't likely to have the muscle to replace that cash during the year—a struggle made all the worse if that year happens to be a down year in the market, as was the case in 2007 and 2008 when the global financial crisis tanked just about every asset at the same moment. Think about it this way: If Mom/Dad withdraw 10% from a $100,000 nest egg, well, that means the remaining assets must grow more than 11% just to tread water. That's asking a lot of an account, given that aggressive, all-stock portfolios can be expected to return, on average, between 8% and 10% in an average year—and no one would suggest a retiree have their whole nest egg in the stock market. That's because if the market craters, and Mom/

Dad's portfolio loses 20% in a year they've already withdrawn 10% to live on, then the remaining portfolio needs to gain 25% to get back to where it would have been after taking out the 10% to live on. That is an extreme feat to ask of a retirement-oriented portfolio. Though the portfolio might achieve that goal, it will only do so because of the risk taken on in pursuit of the higher return, and the higher risk simply exposes Mom/Dad to potentially catastrophic losses.

Financial planners, advisors, actuaries, and others have devised a number of methods to determine how much cash a retiree can prudently draw from a nest egg, and all the various approaches have their pros and cons. We're going to examine a few of them so that you know your options, but ultimately this is a conversation you and your parents should have with a trusted planner or advisor since each family's financial situation and needs are unique and impossible to properly address in a book written for the generic masses.

The Dividends and Interest Solution

For many retirees, the goal historically has been to live off dividends or, more commonly, interest from fixed-income investments such as CDs, savings bonds, municipal bonds, and U.S. government Treasury bonds. The thesis held that by never eating into principal retirees could assure their well would never run dry. That's a noble goal, no doubt, but it's one that's generally unattainable unless a parent has a seriously large stash of cash. Even if you assume interest rates of 5% and a generous dividend payout of 4% (and the dividend paying constituents in the S&P 500 stock index only yielded an aggregate 2.4% at the start of 2010), your parents would need a portfolio of more than $1.1 million, split roughly evenly between stocks and bonds to generate about $50,000 a year. (To calculate dividend yield, just divide a company's annual dividend payment by the company's current stock price.)

Clearly the dividends and interest-only policy is pretty much a nonstarter for most retirees. Indeed, eating into principal is likely a necessity for all but the wealthiest retirees.

Along similar lines, many retirees assume they should stash their nest egg in fixed-income investments because such investments (1) generate guaranteed returns over a prescribed number of years, thereby negating income fluctuation; and (2) provide principal guarantee, thereby eliminating worries that the original investment will wither or disappear. Indeed, CDs and U.S. Treasury bonds offer a rock-solid guarantee that principal will never vanish if the investments are held to maturity. Highly rated municipal bonds and corporate bonds are just a step or two behind on the safety spectrum—although they do carry default risk, or the risk that the municipality or the company runs into financial trouble and can't pay its debts.

Alas, there is a major flaw in this thinking. It's all a false sense of security. Bonds generally do not grow. They are, for the most part, stagnant investments that in most cases pay a set interest rate for x number of years, then return to the investor the same number of dollars that were originally invested. (A caveat: Bonds bought at a discount will return a bit more principal at maturity, while those bought at a premium will return a bit less. See **bond pricing** in the appendix if you really care to understand the explanation for this.) While this so-called safety of principal might sound appealing in an age when stocks and bonds and houses and just about every other asset have proven they can fall in value, traditional fixed-income investments are hobbled by the great bugbear of inflation.

Throughout the time period money is tied up in a fixed-income investment, inflation is eroding the purchasing power of the invested principal. Worse, inflation compounds each year, building upon last year's higher prices so that what cost $1 this year might cost $1.03 next year and then $1.07 in the third year. The fixed interest rate a bond pays out does not compound. The dollar you earn in year one is the dollar you earn in year seven; nothing changes—though the value of that dollar tumbles sharply. Those two factors don't mix well, especially for retirees who face twenty or thirty years or more living off their limited assets.

Consider a real-life example: In 1987, when U.S. Treasury bonds scheduled to mature thirty years later in 2017 were yielding about 8.25%, a retiree might have sunk an entire $500,000 nest egg into Treasury debt, happy to know the U.S. government would never default on that debt—meaning all $500,000 would return one day—and content with the $41,250 a year those bonds kicked off. But remember: That $41,250 is fixed for the duration; it doesn't change through the years.

The result is that by 2010, twenty-three years after investing in those Treasury bonds, that $41,250 in annual income has the spending equivalency of just $22,000 based on the real inflation—roughly 3% a year—that occurred during that stretch. The interest income provided by the bonds never changed, but inflation gnawed away nearly half the retiree's purchasing power.

As such, while bonds and the stability they offer certainly have a place in every retiree's portfolio, recognize that a portfolio built singularly of bonds and CDs is all but destined to fail over time because a fixed rate of return is no match for even mild inflation. Thus, aiming to rely on dividends and interest only is generally not a workable system.

The 4%–Maybe 5%–Solution

In what is widely regarded as one of the most definitive studies on retirement income, a trio of professors from Trinity University in San Antonio, Texas, examined historical stock and bond returns between 1926 and 1995 in an effort to determine an initial withdrawal rate that has the highest probability of stretching a nest egg for the longest possible time without a retiree running out of money. The term "initial withdrawal rate" refers to the sum of money withdrawn from a nest egg in the first year of retirement and is typically expressed as a percentage—i.e., 4% of the overall portfolio, for instance.

Though the professors published their conclusions back in 1998, in the *Association of Individual Investors* journal, their research—known simply as the Trinity Study—remains a bedrock of retirement planning today. The conclusion held that a retiree should withdraw about 4% of a nest egg in the first year and then adjust that amount for inflation in subsequent years. It works like this:

- Your parent has $500,000 in investable assets split between stocks and bonds (the ratio works with a variety of stock/bond allocations, though you generally want to stick to a range like 60% stocks/40% bonds or 50% stocks/50% bonds).

- Your parent would then withdraw 4% of $500,000—or $20,000—to live on in the first year this strategy is in place. This $20,000 would be on top of whatever Social Security and any pension plan provide.
- If inflation during that first year runs at, say, 3%, then the withdrawal rate for year two is ratcheted up to $20,600, a 3% raise. Inflation, in terms of this strategy, is determined by the **Consumer Price Index**, which the federal Bureau of Labor Statistics publishes monthly and is also widely available in the media and on the Web.
- Going forward, each year's withdrawal is increased to match the inflation rate. If inflation doesn't move, income doesn't move.
- If inflation runs higher than the portfolio's return for that year (meaning inflation is, say, 7% and the portfolio's total return for the year is just 5%), the withdrawals continue to match inflation.

The general idea is that by hewing to a relatively low initial withdrawal rate, a portfolio of stocks and bonds will last through as many as thirty years—possibly longer—in retirement. Returns generated by the portfolio, particularly the stock component, will help replenish the money being withdrawn, though in some bad years the withdrawals will exceed what the portfolio earns.

Now, to be fair, the Trinity Study does spark controversy among planners who argue that a properly managed nest egg can kick off more than 4% for a retiree to live on. The so-called Jarrett Study (and I promise I won't mention another study) found that a 50/50 split between stocks and bonds could survive a withdrawal rate of about 5.06% and last for three decades. (If you really want to see all the numbers and how they change based on different mixes of stocks and bonds, I encourage you to Google both the Trinity and the Jarrett studies. Much has been written on them in the mainstream financial media.)

All of this isn't to pick sides but to make bold note of this reality: *Portfolios are not likely to endure if the withdrawal rate much exceeds 5%.*

The reason: Investment returns do not move in a straight line. They bounce all over the place. They can be up one year, down another—flat for two or three years in a row. Such gyrations have a direct impact on a portfolio, particularly at a moment when Mom/Dad is draining that portfolio to generate retirement income. If the portfolio were assured of earning 8% a year like clockwork and inflation didn't exist, then a nest egg could support an annual withdrawal of 7% and always replenish itself. But, again, investment markets and the economy don't function that way. Imagine what happens if your parent withdraws 7% in a year when stocks fall 47%, as the Standard & Poor's 500 stock index did in 2008? Even if stocks only comprised half of an overall portfolio, your parent is pulling out a large percentage of the portfolio to live on even as the overall value of the account is tumbling— a double whammy that drains the account even faster. And to make this example even more dramatic, you have to stop to think about how percentages work: A 47% fall does not mean the stock component of the portfolio needs to earn 47% the next year to break even. It means stocks need to earn nearly 89% the next year to claw back to their previous starting point. That's simply not going to happen. Your parent will either face draconian cutbacks in income, or will run out of money many years sooner than expected.

Therefore, work with your parents to set the bogey at a

withdrawal rate of 4%–5% annually, adjusting for inflation as each year passes.

> **TIP:** If you want your parent's nest egg to last longer, in years when the portfolio suffers a loss, have Mom/Dad skip the inflation adjustment for the following year. In applying this rule, the annual withdrawal doesn't deplete the account as much as it otherwise would, allowing the foregone income to remain in the nest egg, where it has an opportunity to grow. That will ultimately help the total portfolio remain viable longer.

Retirement: A Production in Two Acts

THE THING ABOUT RETIREMENT is that it's not homogeneous from one year to the next. In most cases, new retirees are more active than older retirees, and, as such, new retirees have greater spending demands. That needs to factor into Mom/Dad's income requirements.

The two primary pressures of retirement spending—meeting early spending desires yet insuring financial longevity—are exacerbated by the fact that the typical household headed by someone between the ages of fifty-five and sixty-four has somewhere between $75,000 and $100,000 in various types of personal and retirement savings, depending on what study you believe. That's not a lot of money in the grand scheme of retirement, and it won't spin off much money at a withdrawal rate of 4% or 5%. At the high end, $100,000 in income-generating assets, your parent is looking at first-year annual income of $4,000 or $5,000 with which to supplement whatever Social Security income exists. That sum isn't meaningless, but it might not be nearly enough for a parent to live on.

To address the needs of parents with more modest assets, we can split retirement into two distinct acts and fund them separately in an effort to both increase income in the early years (that's Act 1) and then to assure a permanent stream of income in the final years, no matter how long those final years prove to be (that's Act 2).

Act 1 covers the first twenty years of retirement, basically from age sixty-five to eighty-five. Of course, depending on when you're pulled into your parent's life you can alter the time frame to cover fewer years, or you can extend the end date so that if you're pulled in when Dad is, say, seventy, you'd stretch the coverage period to age ninety. During this two-decade stretch— Act 1—a parent commits to spending 85% of a nest egg. The remaining 15% goes into a five-year certificate of deposit that will be rolled over every time it matures during Act 1.

The aim of Act 1 is to bring in a larger chunk of money in the first year, and slowly ramp it down over the next four years, and then slowly ramp it back up again over years seven through eleven, and then back down again through year twenty. This strategy has the effect of providing a beefier amount of income early on, then scaling it back as a parent's lifestyle slows down, and then scaling it back up again just as increased health care costs are likely to arrive. The hope is that the nest egg's returns will be large enough in the years when the withdrawal rate is lower so that the assets still at work can replenish the account to some degree. And just to be clear, when you're talking about the unknowable variables in retirement planning, success is always predicated on some form of "hope" when you don't have a sufficient nest egg, regardless of all the math you'll see trotted out by financial pros.

Act 2 begins around age eighty-five, or possibly a bit later depending on when you helped your parent originally put a plan into place. The aim during this phase is to create a permanent stream of income that a parent can never outlive, no matter how long that is. This is where you deploy that 15% of the nest egg originally parked in a CD back when Act 1 began. Add the cash in the CD to whatever balance remains in the nest egg when the first twenty-year period ends. With the combined funds you purchase an immediate annuity structured to pay out over your parent's remaining life. In doing so, you have created a permanent paycheck that will give you and your parent a sense of security in knowing that the money will never run out.

If the annuity and Social Security don't provide enough income, your parent can take out a **reverse mortgage** on the family home, assuming Mom/Dad still owns a home. Like an immediate annuity, a reverse mortgage can be structured to pay out over a parent's remaining life, among other payout options. (Larger sections on annuities and reverse mortgages are coming up shortly.)

Here's an example of how the two-act plan might look, using a starting nest egg of $100,000, of which $85,000 goes into a portfolio split 50/50 between stocks and bonds, and $15,000 goes into a five-year certificate of deposit at a local bank or credit union. This chart is based on real returns generated between 1990 and 2009 by the Standard & Poor's 500 stock index and the benchmark Lehman Aggregate Bond Index. The interest earned in the CD is based on rates prevailing at the time for five-year certificates.

Stock and Bond Portfolio

Year	Withdrawal Percentage	Annual $ Drawdown	Aggregate Return	Remaining Balance
1990	10%	$8,500.00	2.93%	$78,741.45
1991	9%	$8,749.05	23.24%	$86,255.13
1992	8%	$10,781.89	7.51%	$81,141.28
1993	7%	$11,591.61	9.92%	$76,445.52
1994	6%	$12,740.92	-0.80%	$63,194.96
1995	5%	$12,638.99	26.53%	$63,965.94
1996	6%	$10,660.99	13.30%	$60,391.85
1997	7%	$8,627.41	21.51%	$62,896.38
1998	8%	$7,862.05	18.64%	$65,289.98
1999	9%	$7,254.44	10.11%	$63,902.93
2000	10%	$6,390.29	1.27%	$58,240.17
2001	9%	$6,471.13	-1.73%	$50,876.03
2002	8%	$6,359.50	-5.92%	$41,881.15
2003	7%	$5,983.02	16.39%	$41,781.83
2004	6%	$6,963.64	7.61%	$37,467.85
2005	5%	$7,493.57	3.67%	$31,074.34
2006	5%	$6,214.87	10.05%	$27,356.61
2007	5%	$5,471.32	6.23%	$23,248.74
2008	5%	$4,649.75	-15.88%	$15,645.47
2009	5%	$3,129.09	16.20%	$14,543.40

Certificate of Deposit

	Beginning Value	Annual Interest rate	Ending Value
1st 5 years	$15,000.00	7%	$21,038.28
2nd 5 years	$21,038.28	6%	$28,153.96
3rd 5 years	$28,153.96	5%	$35,932.38
4th 5 years	$35,932.38	5%	$45,859.83

In this particular example, the result of the two-act strategy is that a parent reaching the second act will have about $60,400 to invest in an immediate annuity (the $14,543 remaining in the stock and bond portfolio, and the $45,859 in the CD). And based on 2010 data, an immediate annuity of that size would generate as much as $825 a month to help supplement Social Security income. Best of all, that's income that cannot be outlived; the checks will arrive every month for as many years as the beneficiary is alive.

Now for the giant disclaimer: This example takes just a single period in time, and it was in many ways a unique period in U.S. financial markets; the S&P recorded some of its best consecutive gains ever, and the bond market was in long-term rally mode for much of this period because interest rates were coming down almost continually (and falling interest rates are great news for bonds). Going forward, there's clearly no guarantee a similar environment will emerge.

And, finally, this two-act approach is *not* standard retirement income management. Nevertheless, this strategy serves as an example of how to at least think about generating sufficient income when parents have a modest nest egg to begin with.

Living One Year at a Time

NO MATTER HOW YOU and your parent determine how much to pull from a nest egg annually, make each year's withdrawal at the first of the year, pulling out of the portfolio the entire year's worth of cash all at once. The reason is simple: You want absolute assurances the money needed to live on for the year is out of risk-based assets and stuffed into the rock-solid security of a federally insured bank account. This way, you erase worries that a downdraft in the stock or bond market— or both—will impact the year's withdrawal.

But you still want that money working as best it can to generate some additional income for parents. To that end, you want to split the cash into four different buckets. The first quarter of the money goes into Mom/Dad's checking account; this is the cash parents will spend during the first three months of the year. The remaining three-quarters of the money is divided into three certificates of deposit, each holding a quarter of the original withdrawal. The first CD matures after three months and represents the cash that will fund months four, five, and six. The second CD matures after six months to pay for the costs of months seven, eight, and nine. And the third CD matures in the ninth month to pay for the last quarter of the year. This is known as "**laddering**," and we'll cover this in more depth in just a bit. But the basic idea is that in structuring the funds this way your parent is able to generate the most income possible. Three-month CDs pay more interest than do checking accounts, and six-month CDs pay more than a three-month CD, and the nine-month CD will pay the most.

You'll probably want to set up the CDs so that the income they generate each month flows directly into your parent's checking account, making the funds available for spending needs in the moment rather than becoming available only after each CD matures. To be sure, with modest CD values, the increased income won't afford a new car, but a few extra dollars here and there can help make an expense for a prescription or an electric bill a little easier.

This is, by the way, another instance where you'll want to spend some time shopping around for the best yields you can find locally, often at a credit union, or at an online bank. If you're going to put money to work, might as well make it work as hard as possible.

Increasing Income

GENERATING THE MOST INCOME in the safest fashion from a nest egg is the holy grail of retirement income planning. Everyone, obviously, wants their dollars to stretch as far as possible without taking on much risk.

There are ways to do that for those who are savvy about shopping around for their investments. We've already covered one of the major strategies for accomplishing this: waiting to take Social Security at an older age. But there are other strategies to consider as well, including tweaking the mix of stocks and bonds in a portfolio (which is the riskier approach); using certificates of deposit more efficiently; putting a chunk of a parent's nest egg in an immediate annuity; pursuing a reverse mortgage when a parent owns a home; or, if health allows it, encouraging Mom or Dad to work part time.

Investments

Stocks

Stocks are so-called risk assets, meaning you put money at risk in hopes of generating a return higher than you can get with a riskless asset such as a bank CD or, more commonly,

U.S. government bonds. For that reason, too many retirees who do not rely on professional money managers tend to shy away from stocks for fear of losing their principal. Better to be ultrasafe than devastated by a dramatic downturn in the financial markets that vaporizes a portfolio. That's an understandable fear, particularly among retirees who have a limited nest egg and no working days left to replenish it.

However, given the potential length of time a modern retiree will spend in retirement these days, a nest egg really demands some exposure to stocks in order to survive for as long as a retiree does. Remember that section on inflation and relying too intently on fixed income? You really don't want to find your parent in a situation where, in the pursuit of total risk aversion, Mom/Dad end up with a portfolio that is so incapable of competing with inflation that it cannot support even a modest lifestyle in later years.

This is not an argument for investing in high-growth Internet stocks and the shares of biotechnology companies with unproven medications. No retiree needs exposure to the market's riskiest stocks. However, it is an argument for owning stable, blue-chip companies, particularly those that pay dividends. These are big, brand-name firms that have a long history of growing their business year after year and that in many cases have an equally long history of spinning out a healthy stream of dividends—companies like Pfizer, one of the world's largest makers of pharmaceuticals; burger giant McDonalds; Walmart, the largest retailer on the globe; medical products maker Johnson & Johnson; petrochemical behemoth ExxonMobil; or Coca-Cola. Mind you, those aren't recommendations of stocks you should go buy for your parent's portfolio. Rather, they're examples of the kinds of companies that make for relatively stable, dividend earning investments.

Indeed, the best advice for the bulk of retirees is to own blue-chip stocks through a mutual fund, preferably something like a dividend or income fund, where the portfolio manager's aim isn't to shoot out the lights in the quest for capital appreciation but, rather, to own investments that along with modest growth prospects pay out a stream of dividends or other forms of income. You can research mutual funds online for free at Morningstar.com. Seek out funds that:

- have a solid, longer-term track record of beating whatever index it benchmarks its performance against;
- have a risk profile that is "average" or below;
- provide an annual yield that exceeds whatever the current yield happens to be on the S&P's 500 at the moment; and
- when possible, are guided by a portfolio manager whose tenure is responsible for the long-term record.

At the time of this writing, funds like the Eaton Vance Dividend Builder A and the Putnam Asset Allocation: Growth Y generally fit that bill. Of course, that doesn't mean they'll necessarily fit the bill when you read these words, so, again, those aren't necessarily recommendations. Do your own homework before choosing a fund, since it's easy to do online. Or hire a financial planner by the hour to do it for your parents instead.

TIP: If your parents are using a stockbroker or a financial planner, or if they plan to use one, be sure to vet the person to be as certain as you can that they're not going to use Mom/Dad as an ATM.

Though the great bulk of brokers and brokerage firms are upstanding, brokers and other financial pros are routinely reprimanded by state and federal regulators, or even barred from the securities industry, because of despicable tactics they employ to effectively rob retirees. It's critical, therefore, that you conduct a background check on these people so that you and your parents are informed consumers.

Contact the local securities regulator in your parent's home state (do this with a Google search of "securities regulator" and whatever state your parent lives in). Request a CRD report for the broker who is handling your parent's money. The CRD report—or Central Registration Depository—will detail a stockbroker's past, including, among other items, employment history for the past ten years and any past or pending disciplinary actions by state and federal regulators.

You can also do the search online at www.finra.org, the securities industry self-regulatory agency. Search for "BrokerCheck."

And even if your parent's broker doesn't show up with any violations, always pay attention to brokerage account statements that arrive. If you're not receiving the account statements, request that the brokerage firm send duplicate copies of the statements and the trading slips to your address. Be on the lookout not just for the churning I mentioned earlier in the book, but for missing cash or investments that seem inappropriate for your parent's needs, like, say, a bunch of money moving into a variable annuity or shares of high-risk technology and other such stocks in the portfolio. Brokers make money off the trades they generate and the products they sell, and they clearly have a vested interest in selling into a client's account whatever they can, even if the client didn't request it, doesn't need it, and doesn't benefit from it.

Going global with some greenbacks

This will probably sound much too risky for a retiree, but keep an open mind about it until you get to the end. A retirement portfolio should have a small exposure to overseas stock markets, particularly for retirees early into their retirement.

While foreign stocks are often considered riskier assets than U.S. stocks, when you narrow your focus to developed markets like Japan, Australia, and Western Europe, those shares are, statistically speaking, no more risky than what you find in America. Those markets are stacked with the same caliber of high-quality, stable, multinational behemoths with long histories of success that you find throughout the U.S. economy.

But they offer retirees some advantages that can benefit a nest egg. First, they typically pay meatier dividends (as a percentage of the stock's price), which helps improve a retiree's income. And they offer exposure to the growth happening in other economies, which can offset weakness in the U.S. economy that might otherwise retard the growth of a U.S.-centric portfolio. And potentially more important, putting some money to work in foreign markets exposes a portfolio to other **currencies**. That can be more important than many Americans realize. Many of the products we buy in the U.S.

come to us from other countries—cars from Japan, TVs from South Korea, clothing manufactured in China, frozen seafood from Thailand and Ecuador, even fresh apples and grapes from Chile in the offseason. In periods when the U.S. dollar is weakening against other currencies in the world, those items become increasingly dear here at home, leading to a form of personal inflation that if not addressed in some fashion can leave a nest egg having to work harder and harder to afford life from one year to the next. A weakening dollar has been a long-standing reality as America's financial situation has deteriorated in the past decade or so, and it stands to remain an issue until U.S. lawmakers tackle the staggering federal deficit, as well as the massive financial obligations facing the underfunded Social Security and Medicare systems.

That calls for building some protection into a portfolio. As the dollar weakens, the value of foreign assets rises, even if the share price of that asset goes nowhere. Here's what I mean: Assume Mom owns stock in, say, a German company that is valued at $10,000 when $1 is worth €1. When the dollar falls in value so that $1 is worth, say, €0.65, then that same $10,000 investment is suddenly worth $15,385. The stock went nowhere, but its U.S. dollar value surged dramatically because the dollar fell in relation to the euro. In periods of dollar weakness, that means having to liquidate a smaller piece of a portfolio to generate the necessary income for the year. (In years when the dollar is stronger, you can liquidate U.S. assets and allow the overseas assets to continue growing.)

The additional benefit comes from dividend payments that are supercharged when the U.S. currency stumbles. Assume that same German company paid Mom $500 a year in dividends (a dividend yield of 5%, or $500 ÷ $10,000).

When the dollar falls to €0.65, Mom's dividend income increases to $769.

You don't need to stick a great deal of your parent's money into foreign stocks. It's fine to stick to 5%–10% of the money allocated to the stock component of a portfolio. Stick to mutual funds that focus exclusively on big, developed markets and focus on so-called large-cap stocks, essentially the biggest companies in a particular market. In terms of risk, such mutual funds are little different from owning similar shares in the U.S. market. As of 2010, Vanguard's Total International Stock Index and the Dodge & Cox International Stock Fund were good examples of foreign funds—both offering a history of category-topping returns, a decent yield, and, at least in Dodge & Cox's case, a manager who'd been around for nearly a decade.

Bonds: think local

Even more than stocks, you'll largely want your parent's bond portfolio in a mutual fund, since bonds can be much more challenging to research individually because there's just so many of them. In general, stick to a broad-based, intermediate-term bond index fund (intermediate term because five and ten years tend to be the sweet spot among the various maturity dates for bonds). Bond funds with long-term records of success include Dodge & Cox Income and Fidelity Total Bond. The rules for picking a good stock fund also apply when hunting for a good bond fund, and, again, the two funds mentioned in the last sentence are just examples of good funds as of this writing. Things can change over time.

You also should give municipal bonds some consideration.

These are the bonds sold by the various counties, cities, and agencies within your parent's home state. Most municipal bonds are tax-free at all levels, meaning parents owe no income taxes at a city, state, or federal level on the interest income received. So-called muni bonds generally make the most sense for people in the highest tax brackets, but even with parents in a relatively low tax bracket, avoiding taxes will help boost annual spendable income—and that can be meaningful for retirees on a fixed income looking for ways to generate extra cash.

The caveat with municipal bonds is that in most states you must own local bonds, meaning those issued by jurisdictions within that state. If a parent owns municipal bonds issued by a municipality out of state, then in most cases the parent's home state will apply state and local income taxes to the interest payments, though the income remains tax-free at the federal level.

TIP: In a small number of jurisdictions, all municipal bonds are tax-free, either because the state exempts from taxes the income generated by other states' bonds or because the state imposes no personal income taxes on its residents. Those states and jurisdictions are: Alaska, District of Columbia, Florida, Indiana, Nevada, South Dakota, Texas, Utah, Washington, and Wyoming.

Once again, unless you are working with a financial adviser who is capable of and comfortable with picking individual municipal bonds, the best option is a mutual fund designed to invest exclusively in the bonds issued by the state in which your parents live. Be aware, though, that not all states are represented this way. States with the biggest demand—California, New York, Illinois, etc.—have multiple options. Others have none. In cases where a municipal bond fund dedicated to your parent's state doesn't exist, a broad-based fund can be a substitute, since the income will still escape federal taxes.

One caveat you should understand about bonds and bond funds is that, generally speaking, owning individual bonds tailored to a parent's specific situation is preferable to owning a bond mutual fund. The basic reason is that an individual bond has a preset **maturity date**, so you know exactly when the municipality will redeem the bond. Moreover, with an individual bond you know exactly when each interest payment will be made. Knowing both of those factors allows you to better tailor a bond portfolio to suit income needs. You can, for instance, structure a bond portfolio to provide a smooth stream of income each month, or build it so that income spikes just before the annual homeowner's insurance or property taxes are due, making it easier to afford the expense as it arises.

Bond funds are a different beast entirely, and in that difference bond funds lose some of the safety and assurances that make bonds so desirable in retirement. A bond fund has no set maturity date; bond fund managers are buying and selling bonds constantly and the fund is designed to last into perpetuity. As such, there is no guarantee that the original principal will be intact on the day your parent wants to reclaim the investment. Moreover, it's impossible to structure a bond fund to pay out on a timeline that fits a parent's income needs, assuming that's important.

The convenience of a bond fund's instant diversification, however, is the selling point. A portfolio of individual bonds typically requires at least $100,000 in cash to adequately diversify across at least twenty different bonds in various sectors of the economy. Such a sum implies a much larger overall portfolio when you consider that your parent still needs exposure to stocks and cash. As such, individual bonds are out of the question for most retirees. But, on the chance that your parent has the necessary deep pockets, a portfolio of individual bonds that your parent will hold to maturity is generally a better option.

Laddering CDs

We touched on this briefly a few pages back. To refresh your memory, a CD ladder is essentially a series of certificates of deposit, each maturing at a different point in time.

CDs are standard fare for retirees, and with good reason. The cash is in a rock-solid institution and will never accrue losses. Even if the bank fails—and that was clearly a problem in the 2008–2009 financial crisis, when more than one hundred U.S. banks collapsed—the money is protected by the Federal Deposit Insurance Corporation up to $250,000 per account owner, per bank.

CDs, in particular, are popular because they tend to be the bank products that generate the biggest returns. Their downside, such as it is, comes from the fact that locking in the fattest rates means locking away money for many years, typically five. Short-term CDs often offer rates little higher than those available in a money market account. And that gets to the point about building a CD ladder. The purpose of doing so is to maximize both returns and liquidity, meaning generating the most money from a pool of cash while keeping it locked away for as little time as possible. (And "locked away" is a pejorative term. The money isn't really out of reach. You or your parent could reclaim it anytime before maturity, though the bank will generally impose a fee equal to three months of interest payments.)

You don't need a specific amount of money to ladder CDs. You could, for instance, put $100 in three CDs, maturing respectively in one, three, and five years. In practical terms, however, laddered CDs tend to make the most sense when a parent has several thousand dollars to spread out. That's where you'll see the biggest impact in terms of income. Even if a five-year CD offered 10% and a one-year CD paid 1%, a $100 investment in the five-year CD earns an additional $9.47 in the first year, not much of a boost and certainly not enough of a financial incentive to commit to keeping the money tied up for so long.

With larger dollar values, the increased income is meaningful. With a $50,000 lump sum of cash, a parent has the option to put all of it in a one-year CD so that the money is available fairly readily, or the cash can go into five $10,000 CDs laddered across one-, two-, three-, four-, and five-year periods, with some of the cash fairly readily available, and some of the cash locked up for a number of years. If a parent is clearly going to need the cash in short order, then all the money in a single, one-year CD makes a lot of sense. But if there are no impending needs for a lump sum, then splitting the money across multiple CDs makes more sense.

Consider this scenario, based on prevailing interest rates in early 2010, in which a one-year CD paid 1.9%, a two-year CD paid 2.2%, a three-year CD paid 2.7%, a four-year CD (an odd denomination that can be a challenge to find) paid roughly 3% and a five-year CD paid 3.3%. If a parent put all $50,000 into a one-year CD and asked the bank to deposit the monthly income into a checking account for spending needs, the cash would generate about $79 a month in interest payments.

Spread the same $50,000 across five $10,000 CDs that mature in one, two, three, four, and five years, and the monthly income in the first year exceeds $109. To get the same return from a single CD means locking the entire $50,000 up for three years. There's nothing particularly wrong with that if your parent won't need access to the underlying principal during that three-year stint. But even if access to principal isn't an issue, a ladder still makes more sense because of the way it continues to function.

CD ladders are designed to maintain the original time horizon. In other words, if you have a number of CDs spread out across five years, then the ladder always maintains that five-year structure. (Of course, a ladder could cover one year or three years or whatever time frame you want.) To effect this, you roll each maturing CD into a new five-year CD. If that doesn't make obvious sense to you, think about it this way: As the one-year CD matures, the two-year CD, which has been paying out for the past year, now has just one year remaining before maturity. It has effectively become a one-year CD. The three-year is now a two-year, and so forth. Thus, to keep the integrity of a five-year ladder you need a new five-year CD, since the one currently in place is now down to four years.

The ultimate benefit of this is that in rolling into a new five-year CD, your parent can capture any higher interest rates that are prevailing at that time, which will serve to boost income even more. To give a dramatic example, suppose inflation heats up during the first year the ladder is in place. Parents locked into a three-year CD will earn their roughly $109 a month in interest income, just like parents in the laddered CD would. But as year two begins and you roll that first maturing CD into a new five-year CD now paying 6% (remember, inflation kicked in), your parent is now earning $143 a month in interest payments, a nice bonus for someone living on a fixed income.

And if your parents aren't living on the interest income and are, instead, allowing it to collect inside the CD, then the ladder simply means a bigger stash of cash to draw on one day or to bequeath to heirs.

Finally, as with any bank product, shop around for the best rates—locally and online. Though CDs are a fairly commoditized product, banks can be aggressive in pricing them. If a bank for whatever reason is trying to draw in cash, it might decide to offer the best rates on a two-year CD, while another bank down the road really wants five-year money and prices its five-year CDs better than the competition. As a consumer trying to pump up your parent's monthly income, it's all about shopping for the best rates you can find.

TIP: If parents have more than $250,000 on deposit at a single bank, make certain the money is split into different accounts and titled appropriately so that every dollar is insured.

If both parents are alive, then both a joint savings account and joint checking account can each hold $250,000. On top of that, each parent could own individual savings and/or checking accounts, each holding a combined $250,000. In all $1 million is covered by the FDIC at that bank. It looks like this:

Mom/Dad joint checking: $250,000
Mom/Dad joint savings: $250,000
Mom individual checking/savings: $250,000
Dad individual checking/savings: $250,000
Total coverage: $1,000,000

If only one parent is still alive, then the sum of all the accounts held at a particular bank cannot surpass $250,000. If a parent has more money in a bank than is covered, you either have to split the money across multiple banks or open a joint account in your and your parent's names, which will provide additional coverage for that account.

If you want help determining what cash is and isn't covered at each bank, check out www.myFDICinsurance.gov. It provides a calculator that determines whether any account balances you or your parents have are uncovered by FDIC insurance.

Note: Congress increased the limit to $250,000 from $100,000 in the wake of the 2008–2009 financial crisis. Congress was scheduled to roll back the protection to $100,000 at some point, though that hadn't happened as of this writing. In the future it could be rolled back, and if so you'll want to make sure all your parent's bank accounts fall within the bounds of whatever new limit might emerge.

The proper portfolio pix: there's no perfect model

The proper mix of stocks and bonds and cash is the mix that allows you and your parents to sleep at night. That may sound trite, but it is the only true gauge that works. Mom/ Dad can look at all the charts and all the probabilities, but if at the end of the day the mix of assets has them paranoid that a market correction will wipe them out or leave them unable to afford their cost of living, then it is clearly the wrong mix.

Thus, telling you what an appropriate mix might be for your parent is largely impossible.

But there are a couple of generalities and rules of thumb around which you should begin helping your parent structure a nest egg.

- Do *not* put all the money into CDs, savings accounts, and bonds. Inflation will decimate those assets over time and that will not help a parent maintain financial security later in life. Some money in CDs is fine, but research from Ibbotson Associates, an investment research firm, found that the best cash option for keeping pace with inflation is a **money market account** (not the same as a **money market mutual fund**). Money market accounts are bank accounts tied to the so-called prime rate, and the prime rate tends to move in lockstep with federal monetary policy so that when the **Federal Reserve** raises interest rates, the prime rate increases instantly. When the prime rate moves higher, the interest rate on a money market account instantly rises, too.
- Depending on a parent's age, put between 20% and 60% of the nest egg into high-quality, dividend-paying U.S. and global stocks to provide the necessary growth as well as income. Where your parent should be on that spectrum between 20% and 60% largely depends on age.

One of the long-standing rules of thumb in the investment world is to subtract a person's age by some factor, with the result determining the percentage of a portfolio an investor should earmark for stocks. Which factor to use is debatable. Some say 100; some say 120. A researcher in the *Journal of Financial Planning* found that 128 is the factor most appropriate for moderate risk–tolerant investors, meaning that if Mom/Dad is, say, seventy-two years old, then stocks should account for somewhere in the neighborhood of 56% of the portfolio. But, again, tweak that as necessary to match a parent's ultimate comfort level. If Mom/Dad is exceedingly conservative, start with a factor closer to 100, which will necessarily reduce the percentage of money earmarked for stocks. Just don't let the final amount of money in stocks migrate too low, lest the portfolio become incapable of meeting your parent's needs.

If you want a little help working up an asset mix, you can find a variety of asset-allocation calculators all over the Internet. TIAA-CREF, a well-respected financial and retirement services firm, has one that as of 2010 was located at www.tiaa-cref.org. Plug "asset allocation calculator" into the search box at TIAA-CREF's home page.

Ultimately the proper portfolio mix isn't about how parents are allocated among various assets, just that they are allocated in some fashion.

Annuities

Annuities are potentially one of the smartest vehicles for improving and guaranteeing an income stream in retirement. Paradoxically, they're also among the most difficult investment products to understand, one of the most challenging for a consumer to commit to buying, and in certain forms possibly the most abusive investment for retirees when sold by unscrupulous peddlers—and the investment universe is littered with unscrupulous peddlers of annuities.

Nevertheless, a certain type of annuity called an "immediate annuity" can be a brilliant investment for retirees because they can mimic a pension that cannot by outlived. Such a promise works to erase worries that you or your parents might have about Mom/Dad outliving their nest egg.

An immediate annuity is just what it sounds like—an annuity that begins to pay out immediately, usually a month or two after the contract is signed, or at least within the first year. A retiree trades a lump sum of cash to an insurance company in return for a guaranteed stream of income a retiree can structure to last a set number of years, often between five and twenty, or for a remaining lifetime. Payouts can occur monthly, quarterly, annually, or semiannually, depending on what best fits the situation, though most people who buy immediate annuities are typically looking for a monthly paycheck. The payout period, meanwhile, can cover either the annuity owner's lifetime or it can stretch to cover a surviving spouse, for either a specified time or a specified dollar amount after the owner dies.

Which option is best among all the various permutations is highly subjective because each person's needs, situation, and available assets are specific to that life, and are based on what other assets and income are available and a retiree's spending needs and overall health. If you or your parents ultimately opt to pursue an immediate annuity, spend time with a reputable financial planner who is paid by the hour and is well versed in elder finances.

TIP: A deferred annuity—particularly a so-called deferred variable annuity—is *not* a wise investment for a retiree, especially a retiree who is up in years.

Unlike immediate annuities, which are built to provide an immediate income stream in retirement, a deferred annuity is designed as an accumulation vehicle, mainly for people who are still in the workforce and saving for a retirement date that remains several years away. Indeed, most deferred annuity contracts require that the principal remain untouched for between seven and ten years. The elderly generally don't have enough time to benefit from the tax deferred growth of the annuity over a decade.

Worse, deferred variable annuities typically impose surrender fees (penalties) if the contract is broken before the deferral period ends. Though annuity companies are working to improve these types of annuities, the contracts typically impose fees as high as 8%–15% of the underlying value, slowly sliding down to 0% over a number of years. If your parent needs the money during the deferral period, expect to see the account value take a meaningful haircut.

For those reasons, many financial planners, elder law attorneys, law-enforcement officials, and state and federal regulators routinely caution seniors away from deferred variable annuities, noting they are almost universally a bad investment for the elderly.

At any given moment, the returns generated by an immediate annuity are broadly similar to what you'd find with a multiyear certificate of deposit or government bonds. Yet unlike bonds and CDs, the annuity will almost always kick off more spendable income each month. And that's where they can become so useful for creating additional income in retirement.

This bigger paycheck happens because of the way an annuity is designed. The income stream is partly the **return on investment** and partly a **return of investment**, meaning each check is comprised of earnings the principal investment generated as well as some of that original principal. In contrast, bonds and CDs spin out a monthly interest payment only, with the principal returning once the maturity date has been reached. And while that makes it sound like you're ultimately recouping the same amount of money over time, just in a different form of payout, CDs and bonds cannot be structured to guarantee the level of income for life. In other words, your parent might invest, say, $50,000 in an annuity contract and ultimately live so long that the annuity company repays the entire $50,000, plus all the agreed-upon interest payments—and then tens of thousands of dollars more because of how long your parent lived. You will never get that from a CD or bond.

Investing in an immediate annuity, therefore, is effectively creating a pension that can't be outlived. And that's what can make them so appealing, particularly for retirees without enough assets to assure they'll never run out of cash.

What makes them so difficult to buy, however, is the amount of cash they consume. An immediate annuity requires a fairly sizeable investment to create any level of income. In 2010, for instance, an immediate annuity seeded with $50,000 would pay a seventy-year-old anywhere from $275 to $861 a month, depending on how the contract was structured. If that retiree wanted income for life, the sum would be about $360 a month. The younger you are, the smaller the paycheck: At sixty-five, the same retiree would receive $315 a month using the lifetime option; at sixty-two the payment falls to $297. (Annuity contracts fluctuate based on interest rates, and early 2010 rates were exceedingly low. As rates move up, the payments rise accordingly.)

Many retirees reflexively recoil at parting with such a big slug of their money, particularly if that slug represents the bulk of their savings, and particularly because once annuity payments begin, there's no turning back; they can't get the cash back just because they want it, or even if they need it. Rightly, retirees want to feel a sense of financial security, and they see liquid savings as that security.

Yet, an immediate annuity can ultimately provide greater security than the cash because of the lifetime income option. Live long enough and the $50,000 in savings will drain away to nothing. In an annuity, it lives on and on and on, as long as the owner does.

The other big fear retirees have is that instead of living too long they might die too soon—and in doing so will have given an annuity company a bundle of money that will no longer exist to help a surviving spouse afford life or that would have otherwise gone to heirs. In some cases that is true; that's the risk you take when choosing between your money outliving you or you outliving your money. Which is worse: Heirs receiving nothing when a parent dies early, or heirs having to fund that parent's life when the money runs out and Mom/Dad are still alive? (That's not meant to sound callous, only that this is the real-life choice that must be made, and some heirs don't have the financial flexibility to take on the obligation of an indigent parent.)

More to the point, immediate annuities can address this worry of dying too soon. Annuity owners can buy policies that promise to pay a guaranteed number of years, like, say, ten, so that if Dad signs a contract today, and then dies a week later, Mom will still benefit from the contract's payout schedule for the next ten years.

Recognize as well that not all of a nest egg should go into an annuity—and strongly advise your parents to *flee* any pitchman who encourages that. Retirees should never be without immediate access to cash for an emergency, be it a doctor's bill or a car repair or a new air conditioner. Investing all liquid cash in any type of annuity effectively robs a retiree of any financial freedom. At most, no more than 25%–30% of a total nest egg should be allotted to an immediate annuity. (Pitchmen will talk about annuities allowing access to cash, and to a certain degree that can be true with some contracts. But the access is generally limited, so don't buy the arguments. Ask how much of the cash a parent can access, or if there is a limit to how much can be withdrawn in a particular period.)

As well, don't look upon an immediate annuity as the answer to fund all of your parent's financial needs. First off, Social Security will accomplish some portion of that. (And, for the record, Social Security is nothing more than an annuity with built-in inflation protection; in fact it's one of the best you'll find, despite all the knocks against the system.) Instead, employ an immediate annuity to help cover some or all of your parent's fixed costs. Or, depending on your parent's situation, maybe you combine annuity income with Social Security to cover those costs. The idea is to use the permanent streams of income to pay for the permanent expenses that exist, thereby doing away with any worries about Mom/Dad's ability to pay for rent or mortgage, food, insurance, electricity, etc. Income from the remainder of the assets can then fund some discretionary spending.

Immediate annuities can also sport a beneficial tax treatment that can help to boost spendable income. Not to get bogged down in tax law, but that "return of investment" thing mentioned a few paragraphs back is nontaxable income. The government doesn't tax principal, only interest, dividends, and earnings. As such, a significant portion of the annual income an immediate annuity kicks out isn't taxed because it's principal. In a comparison where an investor pulls in an equal amount of income from either a bond or from an annuity, the immediate annuity will ultimately generate more net income because of the tax treatment. The one instance in which this tax benefit doesn't exist is when the principal used to purchase the annuity comes from some sort of tax deferred retirement savings account such as an IRA or a 401(k). The principal inside those accounts was never taxed on the way into the account, so the Internal Revenue Service taxes it on the way out. And just to add another layer of confusion, if the money comes out of a Roth IRA the original concept stands—the principal paid by the annuity isn't taxed because it was already taxed going into the Roth in the first place. I know it seems confusing, but there are so many exceptions and caveats when it comes to financial planning.

At the end of the day, an immediate annuity is one of the best longevity insurance policies you'll find, and it can be one of the most useful tools in the collection of retirement income generators. Mom or Dad will never outlive the cash, the interest and principal lumped into one payment means a larger income stream, and the beneficial tax treatment means that for the same level of monthly or annual income the immediate annuity will provide more money to spend than will other fixed-income investments like bonds or CDs.

Buyer, Beware

Heed this plea: Encourage your parents to consult with you before they ever agree to buy an annuity.

Prepare your parents for the possibility that bankers they trust as well as financial charlatans who try to gain their trust might try to convince them of the benefits of sinking their money into an annuity of one kind or another. Request that your parents do *not* sign any paperwork but instead call you first so that you or a financial pro you trust can take apart the document and decipher the fees, and so that you or the pro can question the salesperson about why this particular product is needed by your parent at this particular moment.

To be sure, not every person selling an annuity is a

rip-off artist; some annuity sales support a legitimate need. But in far too many instances, state and federal regulators have found fraud rampant in the practices of insurance companies behind the annuities being sold or, more frequently, in the ranks of the peddlers who are simply out to generate a fat commission by separating the elderly from their cash.

If you suspect a parent has been scammed into buying an annuity, most states have a rescission period of anywhere from ten days to a month (check with your parent's state's insurance regulator for specifics). During this period the contract can be nullified and all money returned without penalty.

If the contract is past the rescission period, write a stern letter to the insurance company, copying in the salesperson as well as the state insurance regulator, the state securities regulator, the federal Securities and Exchange Commission, and the state banking department if the annuity was sold through a bank. You'll want to liberally spice your letter with phrases such as "a violation of the Know Your Customer rules" and "an inappropriate investment for an elderly investor." There are certain regulations that salespeople and insurers must follow, or else they face potential problems with regulators. Enlist the help of an attorney, if necessary. The letter won't always help, but sometimes it can prompt the right people to act on your behalf to reverse a particularly egregious transaction. Or it might lead to arbitration, through which Mom/Dad might recoup some money.

Ultimately, though, it's better to have Mom or Dad call you first to prevent the sale in the first place.

Reverse Mortgage: The Good and the Scary

We're ending this chapter with an income strategy—the reverse mortgage—that segues nicely into the next chapter, "The House." Though it's clearly house related, a reverse mortgage is tied to housing only to the degree that a house is required as part of the transaction. In practical terms, a reverse mortgage is an income generation vehicle and, as such, must be part of a chapter discussing the finances of retirement.

Reverse mortgages have gained a tremendous following among older homeowners, who are the sole target audience. The federal Housing and Urban Development agency reports that retirees signed up for roughly $30 billion in reverse mortgages in the 2009 federal fiscal year. A decade earlier the product barely registered. Retirees have flocked to reverse mortgage because of what they offer: a way to turn an illiquid asset—equity locked up in the market value of a house—into a stream of income that can help afford in retirement everything from vacations to medical bills to long-term care insurance premiums.

At the same time, however, a reverse mortgage is an expensive way to generate income. Moreover, reverse mortgages are ripe for abuse because they mix a big sum of cash with the elderly, a cohort that financial sleazebags target with dodgy tactics to generate fear and effectively steal the money. And while a reverse mortgage can be a useful tool, it is not for every retiree. So don't let a parent rush into a reverse mortgage, and don't rush to push them into one without everyone understanding the costs and risks.

In a nutshell, a reverse mortgage works like a traditional mortgage only in reverse. Instead of taking out a mortgage to buy a house, retirees use a reverse mortgage to take equity out of their house. Think about it this way: With a traditional mortgage, a homeowner sends a check to the bank each month, and each payment *increases* the equity in the home. With a reverse mortgage, the bank sends the homeowner a check, and each payment *decreases* the equity in the home.

Those payments Mom/Dad receive from a reverse mortgage can be structured either as a lump sum, monthly installments, a line of credit for which the unused portion grows larger each year, or a combination of line of credit and monthly payments. If a retiree chooses the monthly payment option, those payments, as with an immediate annuity, can be structured to continue for a prescribed number of years or—and this is the good part—for as long as the retiree lives, even if that means the lender ultimately pays out thousands of dollars more than the home is actually worth.

To qualify for a reverse mortgage, an applicant must:

- be at least sixty-two years old (and if a couple applies for a reverse mortgage together, they both must be at least sixty-two);
- own the home as a primary residence, and this can be a single-family home, a qualified townhouse or condominium, a manufactured home or a one- to four-family owner-occupied property.

As part of the reverse mortgage process, retirees *must* sign up for a financial counseling session. It's mandated by the government, and it must be provided by a counselor independent of the lender. This session ensures that the homeowner fully understands the ramifications of the reverse mortgage and reviews whatever alternative sources of funding a retiree might have access to in order to achieve the same financial goal.

If your parents are still paying on a traditional mortgage, it is paid off as part of the reverse mortgage process. Your parents then have access to a portion of the equity in their home—a transaction, you might recognize, that trades a monthly house payment for a monthly income source. That can represent a huge financial swing. If Mom and Dad were paying, say, $1,000 a month on a traditional mortgage but instead now receive $600 a month from a reverse mortgage, their spendable income has increased by $1,600 a month, which can dramatically reshape their life in retirement and remove a tremendous burden from their shoulders and yours.

One question to consider if a mortgage currently exists on the house: Will the amount a lender is willing to lend cover that existing mortgage and still leave money to supplement a retirement income? Suppose a lender is willing to lend $163,000 on a $250,000 house. If the value of the existing mortgage is $100,000, then that leaves more than $60,000 to supplement retirement income. If, however, the existing mortgage is $170,000, then taking out a reverse mortgage means Mom/Dad must come up with the additional $15,000 from their own nest egg to complete the transaction. In most cases, that probably doesn't make a lot of sense for many people. But in some cases it might. Though the reverse mortgage in this particular instance won't generate any income, it will eradicate the monthly mortgage payment a parent is now making, thus freeing up that cash for other needs. So, in a backdoor way, the reverse mortgage helps to create additional spendable income.

How much money Mom/Dad will get in a reverse mortgage is based on their age, the location and value of their home, and prevailing interest rates. The older the retiree and the lower the interest rates, the larger the cash available. A sixty-two-year-old in 2010 (when interest rates were exceptionally low) living in a $250,000 house in an average American city could expect a reverse mortgage to generate a lump sum of roughly $86,000, or monthly payments of about $560. At seventy-two years old, the same person in the same house would get about $111,000, or $782 a month.

Regardless of the home's worth, lenders will finance only a portion of the value. To get an idea of the amount of money Mom/Dad might be able to generate from their house, play with the reverse mortgage calculator at AARP. (You can find it at www.aarp.org. Search for "reverse mortgage," and on that page you will find the link to the reverse mortgage calculator, as well as a ton of other information about reverse mortgages.)

TIP: Generally speaking, a reverse mortgage doesn't affect regular Social Security and Medicare benefits. However, it can impact Medicaid, which is means-tested. Before applying for a reverse mortgage, arrange to meet with a local attorney who is an expert in eldercare of Medicaid law to make sure you and

Mom/Dad understand the impacts a reverse mortgage might have on Medicaid eligibility, assuming Medicaid is an issue relevant to your parent.

Despite worries that often crop up, a reverse mortgage lender does not own the house. The homeowner continues to own the home, and must continue to maintain the house and pay the necessary property taxes and homeowner's insurance.

The lender only recoups the debt—the accumulated principal and interest—when the home is sold, which can occur when a parent passes away, moves to a new house, or relocates to a nursing home or assisted living facility. Despite misconceptions, a lender will never kick a retiree out of the house, and the accumulated debt can never exceed the value of the house, even if the lender through the years has sent the homeowner checks that exceed the ultimate value of the property. In that case, the lender simply made a bad bet and books a loss. Neither heirs nor the estate are on the hook for any additional money. Moreover, if proceeds from the home's sale exceed the value of outstanding debt, that remaining money goes back to the owner, or the owner's estate or heirs.

Now, for the big question: Does your parent really need a reverse mortgage?

That answer depends entirely on how long your parents intend to remain in the home, their wishes when it comes to the inheritance they want to leave their heirs, and how they aim to spend the proceeds.

If Mom/Dad only expect to be in the house two to three more years, then consider other avenues that might exist, since the cost of the reverse mortgage can be quite expensive.

If Mom/Dad are adamant about wanting to keep the house within the family, or if you and any other heirs want to keep the house in the family, then a reverse mortgage might not make sense. As noted previously, this money must be paid back, and generally speaking that requires the sale of the house, unless you or the group of heirs decide to contribute a bunch of cash to repay the reverse mortgage without selling the house. As such, a big consideration with a reverse mortgage is the potential impact on heirs.

As for the use of the proceeds, some retirees use the money received from a reverse mortgage to pay necessary living expenses or medical costs; that can be a good use of a reverse mortgage because it provides a way for parents to maintain their financial independence without relying on friends or, more likely, family. Some funnel the cash into premium payments for a long-term care policy that will cover their expenses in a nursing home or assisted living center, which, to many peoples' great surprise, are not covered by health insurance or Medicare to any real degree. (More on long-term care in chapter 6, "The Health.") That, too, can be a very smart use of the money, since the increasing likelihood is that a great many retirees will live longer than they expect, and a long-term care policy can provide a much-needed source of funding to pay for the increasingly pricey costs of eldercare, either in the home or in an institutional setting. Again, that takes the strain off of family and provides everyone a certain peace of mind that Mom/Dad's medical needs in the final stages of life will be met.

And some people use reverse mortgage money for consumer expenditures like a car or a vacation, or as a source of funding for investments. Both are terrible uses of the money, and don't let a shady salesman convince you or your parents that this is a valid reason for pursuing a reverse mortgage. Indeed, warn your parents and be prepared yourself: If anyone recommends that Mom/Dad take out a reverse mortgage and put the money to work in an investment product, flee. That's a person looking to make a big commission at your parent's expense.

A reverse mortgage, because of built-in fees that run into the thousands of dollars, and the monthly interest accumulation that will easily run into the tens of thousands over time, is a very expensive means of paying for consumer items. And any sort of relatively safe investment that a reverse mortgage might fund is going to struggle to overcome those embedded costs. Clearly it makes very little sense to borrow high-priced money to stick it into what is likely to be lower-return investments, which will impose their own hurdle in terms of the commission that a selling agent will most certainly collect. That's a losing proposition from the outset.

So, to sum things up:

- If Mom/Dad need a reverse mortgage to supplement income in order to remain in the home, to keep the lights on, and to stay warm and fed, then certainly take a look at a reverse mortgage.

- If Mom/Dad want to put the money into a long-term care policy to secure their future eldercare costs, then, again, at least spend some time weighing the costs and benefits of a reverse mortgage.

- But if Mom/Dad want the money for a vacation, a new motor home, to remodel the kitchen, or if they've been encouraged to take out a reverse mortgage to invest in, say, a variable annuity, a whole life insurance policy, or some other investment product, then a reverse mortgage is generally a bad idea. (One caveat: If Mom/Dad's home is in desperate need of repair, or if hallways and doorways and workspaces in the kitchen and bath must be retrofitted for a handicap, and the only source of adequate funding is a reverse mortgage, then that can be a good use of the cash.)

TIP: Warn your parents to be wary of filling out information cards that arrive in their mailbox, and tell them to decline the invitations that arrive by mail or phone for a free lunch, brunch, or dinner hosted by a local stockbroker or insurance agent.

These are too often the tactics of scammers, who are always finding ways to get seniors to reveal financial information the salesman can exploit in order to separate the elderly from their cash. Here's how they do it:

They send unsolicited letters in the mail from companies

with official-sounding names that often include "federal" or "national," and that fraudulently speak about new government programs targeted at helping senior citizens. They make assertions designed to arouse fear—"Don't let this happen to you!"—or to make seniors think they might be missing out on some government benefit they need to know about—"It's your legal right as a taxpayer!" All that's needed to receive "this valuable free information" is filling out and returning the enclosed informational card. That's all the scammers need to get their foot in the door. Next come the high-pressure phone call and the sales pitch that is guaranteed to leave your parent poorer.

Those free lunches, meanwhile, aren't so free when all is said and done. The local broker/agent is out to accomplish the same thing—gather a lead to exploit later. The lunch is often at a local restaurant or country club, where a local broker or agent will talk about some issue of the day of relevance to seniors, like "How to Stretch a Nest Egg to Ensure a Happy Retirement." At each place setting there will be an informational card, which the speaker points out immediately, asking each retiree to fill it out and hand it in. The card seeks seemingly innocuous information like name, phone number, and biggest fear in retirement.

Therein lies the hook. With that little bit of data, a savvy salesman has all that's needed to make a killing. He knows the name of the person and contact information, and, worse, he knows exactly what each particular retiree fears so that when he calls he can talk about the product he wants to sell in terms that resonate with that retiree's worries. That breaks the ice and gets Mom/Dad thinking, and then it's only a short hop to the sale of an unneeded, high-cost investment product and big commission for the seller.

I know all of this because, as a former *Wall Street Journal* reporter, I have attended seminars where these tactics are employed and schools where salesmen are taught these skills by pros who have so perfected that shtick that one of them bragged to his pupils, "my goal is to walk into a house, find out every dollar these people have, and then walk out with everything they own . . . and I do it every day."

These people are scum. And it's up to you to help protect your parents from such parasites.

5

The House

HOME. FOR THE ELDERLY, it really is where the heart is—
and, often, the heartache.

Trying to convince Mom or Dad to leave the comforts of
a house or apartment they've known for possibly decades can
be one of the more challenging and heartrending exercises in
caring for an aging parent. As the years pile up, people grow
increasingly rooted to where they are. They routinely have
long-standing ties to their little corner of the community, to
their neighbors, their doctors, their friends, the merchants,
banks, grocers, and restaurants they've frequented for years.
They instinctively know their way around the area and generally feel a certain degree of safety in their surroundings.
Little wonder, then, that any talk of upending that security
by moving a parent to a nursing home, an assisted living
center, or some other arrangement that's not their own home
can cause consternation and conflict. You are essentially suggesting that Mom or Dad or both give up all that they know
and all that gives them a sense of comfort. Clearly that can
feel threatening. And because an aging mind can, at times,

react to threats just like a child's mind does, such threats are sometimes met with petulant defiance and anger aimed at the source of this new sense of unease—you.

Still, when parents reach a point when they're no longer capable of functioning on their own, appropriate housing becomes an overriding concern—not just for their safety, but also for your peace of mind.

The primary questions that arise when this moment arrives: What are the options? Which one is best for my parent's situation? What will it cost? And perhaps the ultimate question: Who's paying for all of this?

The easiest part is laying out your options, since they're fairly self-contained. Certainly these aren't the only options; nearly endless possibilities exist to meet the unique demands of each family. But three basic options capture the breadth of possibilities you need to consider:

1. Parents—or their offspring—can pay for a sitter, aide, or nursing service to provide the necessary level of in-home care.
2. Parents can move in with any siblings who might still be alive and capable of providing care, or with any offspring who are willing to assume the obligation of caring for Mom/Dad.
3. Parents can move into a nursing home, an assisted living center, a continuing care retirement community, or some other such facility that provides both shelter and care for the aging.

The rest of the questions are more problematic, and that's where all the challenges arise. Thus, that's what this chapter is all about: examining the three broad options above, and addressing a uniform set of questions for each: (1) what is this option, (2) who is it best for, (3) what are the benefits and drawbacks, (4) how much does it cost, and (5) who pays. This way, you're better equipped to manage the issue of housing for Mom and Dad when the time comes.

In-Home Care

WHAT IT IS: As the name implies, in-home care is care delivered inside the family home. And given the choice, the elderly generally would rather stay at home until the very end, for the very reasons explained at the start of this chapter: comfort, security, and the feeling of independence that is so important as we age. Indeed, AARP, the umbrella organization for retirees, has found in its surveys that the vast bulk of older adults—"vast" as in nearly 90%—want to remain in their own home for as long as possible, what's known as "aging in place."

The services a parent requires at home are provided by a wide variety of potential employees, depending on what Mom/Dad need. Actual health care is the purview of nurses and home health aides. Nonmedical services come from home care workers who provide everything from cooking and cleaning and sitter services, to transporting Mom/Dad to doctors' appointments and shopping.

Of course, aging in place is not always possible, particularly in the presence of medical issues such as Alzheimer's that require specialized care. But to the degree in-home care fits into your family's situation, give the concept due consideration. Not only does it play to the desires of so many aged parents, but the arrangement can also have meaningful benefits for you as well, which we'll get into in a moment.

Who it's for: In-home care is for parents still able to provide for many of their own daily needs. That includes parents who must rely to some extent on regular services offered by home health aides, cleaners, or Meals on Wheels, or even if you or other family members or neighbors must visit regularly or daily to make sure Mom and Dad are doing OK.

Unless you are already intimately familiar with this world, you might be wondering what "able to provide for many of their own daily needs" means. See the sidebar below, "Defining the Activities of Daily Living," for that answer.

Defining the Activities of Daily Living

The term "activities of daily living" is actually a medical term used to measure the ability/inability to care for oneself. Because this term is used throughout the world of geriatric care, you should understand it from the outset. Medical professionals, social workers, and facility directors at nursing homes, assisted living centers, and adult day care facilities will routinely use it in conversations you have with them.

One of the crucial assessments of aging is measuring an elderly person's competency with activities of daily living. These are the basic tasks required of all of us in living our daily lives. Nursing homes, social workers, and insurers providing long-term care coverage use this assessment in making decisions about an elderly person's ability to perform these tasks and, in turn, to determine care needs.

The list of activities is fairly universal from one assessment form to another. They are:

- eating

- dressing

- bathing

- toileting

- transferring (moving from a bed to a chair and back again)

- continence (ability to control bladder and bowel movements)

Insurers and others often use a scale to determine the level of capacity/incapacity with each of these activities. For instance, the Long-Term Care Benefits Assessment Form for one major insurer provides assessors a five-point rating guide, which you can easily adopt to assess your parents yourself:

1. Able to handle activity without assistance.

2. Occasional help needed; less than 50% of the time the activity is attempted.

3. More often than not assistance is required; need help 50%–75% of the time.

4. Most of the time assistance is required; need help 75%–90% of the time.

5. Always or almost always assistance is required; need help more than 90% of the time, or completely unable to perform activity.

As a point of reference, most long-term care insurance policies begin paying benefits when a policyholder cannot perform two of the six activities of daily living. That means if a policyholder rates a 5 for two of the listed activities, they're considered incapacitated enough to necessitate care of some sort, either at a facility or in the home.

The benefits and drawbacks: Perhaps the most significant benefit is simply the fact that you can provide an aging parent's greatest wish: to remain within familiar surroundings.

That, in turn, can make life easier on you because it neutralizes a potential source of friction. Parents, after all, have little reason to argue against the arrangement unless they really do want to move into an assisted living center or nursing home. That will help reduce some of your own stress. In-home care also provides a certain form of leverage in various situations, like, say, if you need to hire a health aide for some level of daily care, and Mom/Dad is obstructing your efforts.

CONVERSATION STARTER:

"Mom/Dad, you've opted to stay at home instead of moving to an assisted living center/nursing home where you'd receive routine care and someone would be looking after your needs all the time. And I'm all for that because I know it makes you happy. But having a nurse or home health aide come by the house to help with various activities you struggle with is critical for [name your reasons]. Of course, this is your choice, though. You can receive the care here at home or somewhere else. So, how do you want me to proceed?"

Yes, that leans a bit into the gray zone of blackmail, and it borders on treating a parent like a child, but it's not as if you're acting in a malicious manner to manipulate your parents. You're trying to provide the service they require in the setting they desire, and sometimes that takes creative debating.

There are other benefits to consider:

- *Costs*: Remaining at home postpones or possibly prevents the need for pricey institutionalized care, and that can sharply reduce the financial impact on your parent's nest egg—or yours, as the case may be. That's not to imply you have no costs or that in-home care is cheap. Depending on your parent's needs you might still have to hire health aides to provide some form of care for some period of time during the day or week, or a housekeeper to maintain cleanliness in the home and to shop and cook a few meals. But the hourly rate charged for those services is likely to be substantially less than the fees required for a nursing home or assisted living center, and the nurse/aide/cleaner/helper isn't generally needed twenty-four hours a day. Additionally, you can find ways to shrink some of those costs by providing some of the necessary care and services yourself, assuming you live close enough to your parents to do so.

- *Maintaining social ties:* Costs aren't just financial; some impacts are social. A study out of Harvard University's Department of Health and Social Behavior found that people with no social ties are at greater risk of cognitive decline than those with five or six social ties. By keeping parents in their home, you help preserve necessary social ties such as those with neighborhood friends or even the postal carrier.

- *Personalized care:* Nothing against nursing home or assisted living center workers, but their job generally isn't to provide one-on-one care to a single patient during the day. They manage a roster of patients. When Mom/Dad ages in place your parent gets the benefit of individual care, which can provide you with some peace of mind.

- *Stress reduction—on you*: Family members routinely feel guilty when putting a parent in a nursing home. They generally feel much better about a situation in which they know Mom/Dad is happy and properly cared for in their own home. Don't underestimate the mental burden of those ever-present thoughts: Is Mom/Dad OK in the nursing home? Did I make the right decision to send them there? How much longer can we afford to keep them there? What happens if they/we/I run out of money? The litany of worrisome questions goes on and on.

As for the drawbacks, you must consider:

- *Worry*: Is your parent *really* all right? You can't be with them constantly, and you might not be able to afford round-the-clock sitters or home health aides, so there will be stretches of time when an elderly parent is home alone. Those are the moments when you worry the most about a slip and fall that breaks a bone or a hip, or any of a wide assortment of potential injuries. Who will be there to help in that emergency? And smaller worries can be just as nagging: Are they eating properly? Is the house clean and well maintained? Is Mom/ Dad keeping up with personal hygiene? Are illnesses/ chronic conditions adequately monitored or are they getting progressively worse without anyone paying attention? Are medications interacting in negative ways, the signs of which are missed when you or others are not around as much as you'd like? In an institutional setting those worries, though they often still exist on some level, are diminished to some degree.

- *Maintenance*: Older homes are more likely to be in physical disrepair and built with old technology and infrastructure. Assuming your parent wants to remain in the home in which they raised the family (or in an older home in general), you're looking at the likelihood the house is rife with issues such as poor insulation that leads to greater energy costs, inoperable windows that lead to potential safety concerns, and a number of chemical, biological, and environmental hazards like asbestos, mice, and mold. Maintenance costs, thus, can be high relative to a parent's fixed income. Moreover, older homeowners routinely put off maintenance and repairs on items such as plumbing, electrical circuitry, and roofs, which leads to safety hazards as well as increased costs, as deferred upkeep begets ever-larger and peripheral problems.

- *Costs:* Just as costs can be a benefit, they also represent a drawback. First, you have the maintenance costs noted in the previous bullet point. Beyond that, though, the family home in which parents want to remain is often much too large for their needs. The upshot is higher-than-necessary costs for heating and cooling a larger-than-necessary house, higher property taxes on a home that's worth more than the value of the smaller house in which your parents should probably be living, and pricier premiums for insuring a bigger home than is required of an elderly lifestyle.

- *Isolation:* A few pages back I noted that aging in place can help a parent maintain social ties, which, in turn, can improve—or at least maintain—cognitive abilities. Yet this, too, can point to a potential drawback. If old friends die or relocate or trusted neighbors move away or even if a longtime postal carrier retires or moves to a new route, a parent's social world at home can collapse, leading to isolation that can leave a parent depressed and susceptible to other ailments and woes. Or it can lead to a desperate parent befriending new people, some of whom may be feigning friendship for nefarious reasons, such as access to an elderly person's finances. The worst part is that you might not recognize the signs of the underlying problems. For that reason, you really need to establish a routine by which you, a trusted friend, a neighbor—someone—regularly reaches out to your parent to gauge personality and mental health. As I noted in previous pages, you might even rely to some degree on a banker with whom your parent regularly interacts.

• *Fraud, abuse, and neglect:* Tying into the isolation concern this drawback stems from the fact that the elderly are much more susceptible to scams and abusive behaviors from caregivers, friends, telemarketers, financial and legal advisors—even family members. When parents are at home alone for long periods during the day, plenty of opportunities arise for lowlifes who victimize the elderly, preying on their fears or manipulating them in other ways. No doubt similar opportunities for abuse arise in an institutional setting. But institutions have many more sets of eyes watching over their charges, greatly increasing the odds that abuses are uncovered.

The finances of aging in place: Every year, the Mature Market Institute inside insurance giant Metropolitan Life reports on the state of eldercare, examining the costs for various types of care that range from nursing homes to assisted living centers to home health care. On an hourly basis, the costs of in-home care are roughly equal to the costs of institutional care. But remember that the point of aging in place is that it is best for a parent who doesn't require round-the-clock institutional care. That's what makes the in-home option substantially less expensive, though "less expensive" is subjective and determined by where in the country your parents happen to live.

MetLife found in its 2009 survey that the cost of care delivered in the home averaged between $19 and $21 an hour, depending on whether you're hiring a home health aide (a more experienced professional or paraprofessional) or a homemaker/companion whose duties typically include cooking, light cleaning, and companionship, but nothing medical. But that's the average. Costs vary widely from one side of the country to the other. For instance, a home health aide in Shreveport, Louisiana, averages about $13 an hour (the low end of the spectrum), while at the high end you're on the hook for $30 an hour, on average, in Minneapolis-St. Paul, Minnesota.

But again, these typically are not costs that you will be paying twenty-four hours a day. In most circumstances you're hiring help for several hours a day, and maybe you or another family member provides care at other hours. You can do the math and see that if you must hire a home health aide full time, you're talking very large dollars, on the order of $240 a day (at the national average), or $1,680 a week—a hefty outlay.

And if a parent who remains at home requires full-time or near full-time care, then strongly consider this tip:

TIP: When hiring full-time aides or sitters, hire more than one to avoid costly overtime. It's cheaper to pay two workers to cover twelve hours in two six-hour shifts than it is to hire one worker to cover the entire stretch, earning normal pay for eight hours and pay at time and a half for four additional hours.

Of course, if Mom/Dad do need round-the-clock care, an in-home setting might not be appropriate to begin with. And even if it is an appropriate option, you should still take a look at institutional possibilities, since on a daily basis nursing homes and assisted living centers can be markedly cheaper than one-on-one care in the home. (For more on in-home care, assisted living, and nursing home costs in your specific area, visit the "Publications" section of MetLife's Mature Market Institute, online at www.metlife.com/mmi.)

Who pays: It depends. In some cases, the costs of aging in place come out of your parent's nest egg—or your pocketbook, if you happen to be paying or helping to pay the bills. In other cases, **Medicare** or **Medicaid** will pay, as will a long-term care contract, if your parent is covered by one of those. (We'll just cover the bare basics here; there's a whole section on these policies coming up in the next chapter, "The Health.")

Let's start with Medicare, a federally administered health insurance plan and one of the more misunderstood programs when it comes to in-home care. People just assume that because they have Medicare they're covered for long-term care needs, and that's not necessarily accurate. When it comes to in-home care specifically, Medicare will pick up the costs of the necessary services at 100%, meaning no out-of-pocket co-payments for you or your parent. And the number of home care visits Medicare covers is unlimited. But there's a catch.

Medicare pays the bills only so long as your parent meets four strict criteria:

1. A doctor must prescribe home care and must devise a plan for that care.
2. An aging parent must require at least one of the following: intermittent, though not full-time, skilled nursing

care; physical therapy or speech-language pathology services; or a continued need for occupational therapy.

3. Your parent must be homebound, meaning that Mom/Dad is normally unable to leave home without a major effort, that leaving home is infrequent and for short periods, and destinations are religious services, medical appointments, and adult day care programs licensed or certified by the state.

4. The Medicare program in the state where Mom/Dad lives must approve the home health agency providing the in-home care.

You must be aware of the caveats:

- Home care coverage *only* falls under Medicare Part A (which covers hospice, home health care, inpatient hospital stays, etc.). The coverage is not provided by Medicare Part B (outpatient services, doctor visits, physical therapy, and so on). So if Mom/Dad doesn't have Part A, then they're not eligible for benefits.
- And Medicare does not pay for custodial care, such as cleaning or cooking.

All of these facts were accurate as of 2010, and Congress is always looking for ways to trim the health care costs it pays. Thus, there's always a chance lawmakers will impose changes that force patients to cover some or all of their home care expenses, or that Congress imposes "means testing" that limits who is eligible for Medicare coverage or the degree to which Medicare will cover various expenses. So check with your local Medicare office to determine the rules when you confront this issue with your parent.

Medicaid is another option. While Medicare is a federal program, Medicaid is a state program, and each state has its own set of rules. Medicaid is actually the country's largest public payer of long-term care expenses, and, thus, pays for some forms of in-home care (you'll need to talk to the Medicaid agency in your parent's home state to determine the scope of coverage).

How Medicaid differs—drastically—is in the qualifications. A senior must effectively be indigent to receive Medicaid benefits, and that won't fit parents who have a certain minimal level of assets. Those levels vary by state and can change from one year to the next, another reason you need to check with the local Medicaid office to determine your parent's eligibility. To give a sense of the eligibility guidelines, the state of New York in 2010 required net income for single people sixty-five years old and older be no more than $767 a month, with total resources of less than $13,800. In North Carolina, the monthly income limit is $903 for the same single person, yet resources cannot exceed $2,000. (Resources generally excluded the value of a house, car, home furnishings, clothing, and jewelry.)

Long-term care policies are another option in a situation where Mom/Dad isn't eligible for Medicare coverage for whatever reason, and where Medicaid isn't a reality because of asset/income levels. LTC policies, as they're widely known, provide financial coverage for the expenses of aging, and that includes nursing homes, assisted living centers, in-home care, and the like. Those costs, as you no doubt recognize from the previous few pages, can grow to a big number quite quickly, and an LTC policy can make those costs substantially more affordable.

The challenge with long-term care contracts is their cost: even for a healthy forty-year-old the annual expense can run to $2,000 or more, and for a retiree who buys coverage later in life the price tag can be much higher. As such, these policies are not affordable to every pocketbook. Also problematic for potential policyholders: LTC is typically sold on a pass/fail basis, rather than being underwritten. When an insurer underwrites a typical policy—for life insurance, let's say—it is pricing the coverage based on the health of the customer, as determined by a physical exam. If the insured person's cholesterol or blood pressure is high, for instance, or if they're a smoker, the insurer prices the policy higher to cover the increased risks.

Not so with LTC. Any health issue that raises a red flag means the insurer will, in most instances, not offer coverage. In effect you are either healthy enough to be insured, or you're not. That, too, means lots of older people won't be able to buy LTC coverage because the moment a frail parent realizes now's the time to seek out LTC insurance is the moment when it's already too late.

All that said, if your parent has the financial means to afford a policy, and is healthy enough to pass the medical exam, then give LTC a look. Many people assume the policies only cover nursing homes, and because the probabilities of ending up in one of those is relatively small, those people often disregard LTC as essentially a waste of money. While that was true years ago, modern policies cover a wide range of end-of-life costs and can help preserve a parent's nest egg or insulate your own wallet. Though there are many poorly designed LTC contracts, the best of them represent very good value for the expense, though you will want to shop around for the best coverage at the best cost.

Finally, there's the pay-as-you-go method to in-home care. With this approach, the costs of end-of-life care come out of Mom/Dad's savings or your own pocketbook.

There's not a whole lot to say here. If Medicare/Medicaid aren't viable options or don't provide sufficient coverage and LTC is too costly, then paying for in-home care must come from whatever financial resources you can cobble together. To help cover some costs, you might be able to find grants and other options through local and federal agencies and community groups. The National Council on Aging offers one of the most comprehensive collections of benefit programs for seniors living on a limited income and with few resources available to them. These programs change all the time, so it would be fairly useless to list them here only for you to find they no longer exist or have changed substantively by the time you read this paragraph. Instead, head to www.ncoa.org and type "benefits access" into the search function, and you'll be taken to the appropriate link. You'll need to input a variety of personalized data, but that's a small inconvenience for locating possible resources that can ease the financial burden of aging.

Questions to Ask and Tips When Hiring a Home Health Care Worker

Start the search for a home health care worker by asking friends, neighbors, coworkers, the congregation at whatever church you might attend, or anyone you know who has had, or might have had, experience with caregivers. Can that person recommend anyone or any agency—or even recommend you don't hire a particular person or agency?

If that turns up no leads, contact a local adult day care facility, social workers at local hospitals, a doctor's office, or assisted living centers. They should be able to point you in the right direction.

When you begin interviewing potential workers or agencies, have a prepared list of questions to ask. This will help you feel comfortable with the hire, and will allow you to define the responsibilities you expect the health care worker to fulfill.

- If going through an agency, what kind of background check does the firm conduct on the health care workers it places with the elderly? You want to know that a criminal background check is routine, that the agency tests for drug use, and that the agency monitors its workers to insure that any required licenses are kept up to date.

- Is the agency or the independent home health worker bonded? If the worker breaks the dishwasher or TV or steals valuables, your parent will be covered for the loss.

- Is the agency/independent worker Medicare certified? This essentially means meeting federal standards for patient care.

- Does the state require any sort of licensing or registration for home care agencies/workers? If so, are those in order? State laws vary, so before you conduct your interviews, call the local Area Agency on

Aging in your parent's community and ask what licenses or registrations are required. This way when you ask the question in the interview you'll know if someone is lying to you.

- What services are included? You want to be sure you understand the scope of services the agency/worker can provide so that you can match those against your parent's needs. We're talking about everything from nursing and certain types of health care, to cooking, cleaning, driving, even walking the dog, if that's necessary.

- How will sick days and vacation days be handled? If going through an agency, will the agency automatically dispatch a replacement? If contracting through an independent worker, does that person have a backup who can step in and temporarily take over the duties of caring for your parent?

- What forms of payment are acceptable? Cash is generally accepted universally, and some long-term care plans pay out in cash. But other LTC plans, as well as Medicare/Medicaid, typically require the home health agency/worker to bill the LTC insurer or the Medicare/Medicaid agency directly. If the home health agency/worker doesn't directly bill insurers, and if you're not paying cash, then you'll need to keep looking. Hiring an in-home caregiver can have tax implications since you or your parent are acting in the capacity of employer, so check with a tax pro to make sure you understand the implications.

- Seek a list of references. Sure, you'll probably only get a list of happy customers, but even the happy ones can be a source of useful information about challenges and issues they might have had.

- If using an agency, what type of supervision does it provide? You want to know the agency is checking up on its workers—a form of quality control that can help ease the worries you will naturally have about leaving Mom/Dad under a stranger's care for several hours a week.

- If a worker will be driving Mom/Dad to a doctor's visit or to go shopping, get a copy of the driver's license as well as proof of insurance. And if the worker will be driving Mom/Dad's car, you need to check with your parent's auto insurer; chances are you'll need to add this person to the coverage, though that might be cost prohibitive. Better to check and know the facts before letting the worker behind the wheel, only to find out after an accident that the insurer does not cover such an occurrence.

Before making a hire, invite the worker to Mom/Dad's house to gauge how the personalities mesh. This sounds goofy, but if your parent has a pet, particularly a dog, pay attention to how the animal reacts. Dogs can be very protective of their owners and they have a good sense of people with whom they come into contact. So don't disregard an animal's negative reaction to certain people.

Finally, after hiring a home health worker, make a habit of randomly stopping by your parent's house for a surprise inspection. Don't announce it's an inspection, of course; come up with some reason to be there, even if it's just "I wanted to say hi to Mom." Alter the days and the time of day you stop by, and don't call to announce that you're on your way over. You want to see what's really occurring when the worker has no clue you're nearby.

Moving in with Siblings or Offspring

WHAT IT IS: Exactly what it sounds like: Mom/Dad take up residence with any brother or sister they might have, or with you or one or another child, if any others exist.

Siblings know each other and, in theory at least, have an underlying affection for one another that can make for a roommate situation that is palatable for everyone involved. The same thesis holds for living with offspring.

In either situation, concerns you might have about a parent's safety, comfort, and loneliness when they're living at home alone can melt away when Mom/Dad instead moves in with you or one of their own siblings. You know the care is authentic and loving.

Potentially, then, this can be a fine, affordable solution when a parent can no longer manage the activities of daily living alone. Clearly, though, you cannot make a unilateral decision to move Mom/Dad in with you or with one of your parent's siblings. Mom/Dad has a say and must be on board, as does the person with whom your parent would live. And if you're talking about bringing Mom/Dad into your own house, then your spouse, assuming you have one, must be involved in this decision as well, otherwise you're creating a potential conflict that could strain your marriage or tear it apart.

Who it's for: Any parent who doesn't want to remain at home alone, especially in instances where Mom/Dad—or you—don't have enough financial resources to afford in-home care or an assisted living center; and when your parent isn't mentally prepared yet for a nursing home.

This arrangement is not right, however, for parents with Alzheimer's or dementia. Such medical conditions often demand a level of care and oversight that goes beyond what an aging sibling or you can offer. And it's not right in situations when personalities will clearly conflict. That will lead to mounting animosities that can cause no end to the headaches you will have to manage.

I've seen that in my own family. My grandmother and my great-aunt (my grandmother's sister) live together. They're in their late eighties, and the conflicts and stresses are huge. They love each other; they care for each other; but they are two entirely different personalities that clash. The conflict that results has been an ongoing theme for the three decades they've been under the same roof. So I can tell you from very personal experience: Be careful who you match your parent with. The pairing might seem obvious, but the end result can create additional stress in your life as well.

Assuming Mom/Dad's sibling is on board with the plan, or that you and your spouse agree this is the best approach, talk to your parent and explain the idea.

CONVERSATION STARTER

"Mom/Dad, I've been thinking about a way to provide you with in-home care that doesn't have such a big impact on your money—and I want to get your thoughts on this. You know that Aunt Millie lives by herself, and she has plenty of room in her house. I talked to her about the idea of you moving in with her, and she's all for it. It would help reduce her costs and it would mean you don't have to pay nearly as much to hire someone to help you during the day . . . and she'd be around all the time instead of just a few hours a day. I see a lot of benefits, but are there any downsides that you see?"

Then, *listen* to the answer. Pay attention to any concerns or hesitancy you hear; don't brush them aside as minor just because this option is the most convenient for you or the family at this particular moment. You don't always have a complete picture of the emotional ties between siblings, and you could be forcing a situation that is untenable for reasons you don't know about and that your parent might not be willing to talk about.

Moreover, you need to independently gauge for yourself if this pairing makes sense. Parent and sibling may eagerly agree to your proposal, but that might just be because they're each lonely and they relish the idea of a roommate to provide comfort and companionship. While that sounds perfect on the surface, underneath the combination of two frail bodies can create more problems than it solves. If an aging sibling already struggles to manage her own daily life, injecting an equally frail body into that calculus will only compound the troubles for both people.

To the degree that you can, take your emotions out of the scene and assess the arrangement as an impartial observer: Does Mom/Dad's sibling honestly have the faculties and the capacity to direct the daily care of your parent? Will doing so create undue strain in the combined household? If you sense that Mom probably shouldn't live with Aunt Sally, then your gut is telling you this might not be such a grand idea, even as your head tries to convince you of the expediency of the strategy. If you find you can't gauge the situation dispassionately, enlist the services of a local social worker or elder-care nurse. By looking at the arrangement as an outsider and assessing the needs of Mom/Dad and the capabilities of the sibling, a qualified third party can help you make the appropriate decision. To find local social workers, nurses, or others who can help you make this assessment contact your local Area Agency on Aging.

The benefits and drawbacks: Perhaps the most important benefit with this arrangement is cost. If you or your parent don't have the money to pay for in-home care, and other options aren't available for whatever reason, an arrangement whereby another family member steps in can be the equivalent of finding a life preserver on stormy seas.

But there are other benefits to consider:

- *Peace of mind:* When a parent is living with you or another family member, your level of worry is reduced—though not necessarily eliminated—because you know there is a certain level of trust, comfort, care, and concern that naturally springs from a family relationship.
- *Proximity:* Just as you grow up to be someone interesting, so do parents. They're often not the same people

you know or remember from your youth, when they are acting more like, well, parents rather than friends. Age mellows people, and when they're suddenly around you every day Mom/Dad can turn out to be pretty cool people you enjoy being with and getting to know in an entirely different way. That can make your time later in life with your parent a truly special period.

- *Built-in babysitter*: Having Mom/Dad living at home can help you and your spouse better manage the necessities of caring for your own kids, and that can help you save money if you have to pay a school or a sitter to watch over your children in the afternoon while you're still at work. Mom/Dad can serve that need, assuming they're still capable. Similarly, having Mom/Dad around exposes your children to their grandparents, creating a bond that otherwise might never have occurred—a benefit not only to the child, but also to your aging parent. It also teaches children how to care for others, giving them life skills that will be important as they build their own relationships and that could come back to benefit you when you're old and no longer capable of managing on your own; you might need to move in with your own children.

- *Reduced logistical headaches*: When a parent is living with you or another family member, travel arrangements for doctor appointments and other necessities are much easier to coordinate. It might still impinge on your work and family life, but it can be far easier to deal with and consume less time than when you're coordinating with sitters or drivers or even neighbors.

As for the drawbacks:

- *Proximity*: Yes, this street runs both ways, because just as proximity to Mom/Dad can be a great way to spend quality time with a parent, it can also be a disaster in some cases. People don't always change for the better, particularly if the early stages of dementia are emerging. Sometimes they become excessively angry and bitter and ornery. You could find that the happy, comedic, fun-loving parent you remember has, because of illness or age, turned into a curmudgeonly, ill-tempered tyrant who runs roughshod over your family and your way of doing things. Moreover, living with aging parents can reveal the small frustrations that on a daily basis grow into the habits that drive you crazy, in turn leading to fights and arguments, all of which will spill over into the rest of your family life, resulting in tension and animosity all around.

- *Costs*: We're talking here about money as well as the mental and physical costs. With Mom/Dad under your roof, you're suddenly responsible for their care, meaning you're the one arranging doctor visits and coordinating the logistics of getting to and fro. As for money, aside from direct outlays you might be responsible for, like added food and utilities expenses, you might routinely need to leave work early to manage a parent's care; maybe you even cut back your hours to part time to make the arrangement work. In some cases, women caregivers in particular have given up careers to provide the necessary care for Mom/Dad, clearly impacting the family's income and standard of living, and ultimately affecting how much money a couple is able to save for their own retirement. That, in turn, can cause or add to those tensions and frustrations elsewhere in the family.

• *The care itself*: As Mom/Dad ages, you or the sibling/ family member ultimately might not be equipped to provide the appropriate care as it becomes necessary. Again, that can lead to growing frustrations.

The finances: Let's be clear: This is not a free arrangement. Yes, you're going to save a small fortune on the costs of institutional care or in-home care that you or your parent would otherwise pay. But there are still costs—both financial and emotional, some of which we covered in previous bullet points.

If Mom/Dad moves in with a sibling, clearly that sibling should not have to assume the financial burden. Indeed, that sibling might not be able to assume the financial burden. Further, you shouldn't place Mom/Dad in another relative's home on the presumption that the room and board is free.

To that end, whether a parent moves in with a sibling, with you, or with some other family member, you have to consider costs for rent, food, utilities, and transportation. What is a fair figure? That depends entirely upon discussions you have with your parent and the person with whom your parent will move in.

If Mom/Dad is moving in with a sibling who lives alone, maybe a fair figure splits the food and utilities in half. As for rent, I wouldn't suggest splitting a mortgage payment in half, since your parent isn't accumulating any of the equity in the house. Instead, I'd examine what a simple one-bedroom apartment costs in an area where your parent might live, and then use that as the starting point for negotiations with the person Mom/Dad will live with.

If your parent is moving in with you, well, then you have to determine yourself how you want to handle the situation. I would suggest not charging for rent, food, or utilities for a couple of reasons. First and foremost, Mom/Dad didn't impose those costs on you to live with them. Yes, there's a big distinction: Your parents chose to have a child and, thus, had certain obligations for raising that child. Nevertheless, the least you can do is return the favor when your time comes to take care of your parent.

Second, and more important financially, better that your parent's money goes toward covering the big costs such as health care and insurance. That will ultimately help you more than will money for rent, food, and such. The more cash Mom/Dad has to pay for the really important costs of aging, the less the impact on you. Think about it this way: Is it better for your parent to spend $500 a month paying you, or to allocate that money to some form of insurance, be it health insurance or a long-term care policy of some sort, that will cover many, if not all, of the meaningful costs?

Who pays: Some of this is reflected in the answers to the previous question. You, your parent, or the person with whom your parent lives will be responsible for various costs, or at least portions of various costs.

Now, depending on Mom/Dad's medical condition, Medicare or Medicaid are sources of income for health-related costs, as detailed in previous pages. And depending on Mom/Dad's financial condition, Medicaid might spring for some ancillary needs like toileting and bathing, light housework, and even running errands. Again, check with the local Medicare/Medicaid offices where you parent lives to determine Mom/Dad's eligibility and the extent to which the programs can provide assistance, particularly if you or another loved one are providing the care. The agencies won't pay any sort of rental costs, however.

Long-term care policies are an option as well—sometimes. LTC policies are typically structured to pay out a daily benefit, based on receipts that you or the agency providing a service remits to the insurer. However, some policies pay a daily benefit regardless of how the money is spent. So if Mom/Dad's policy provides, say, $75 a day, then that's money that can be used to cover various costs each month, from groceries to utilities to doctor bills to, well, paying rent to you or another family member.

Institutional Care: Nursing Homes, Assisted Living, and Other Options

WHAT IT IS: As the name suggests, institutional care is the care provided in an institutional setting. When most people hear "institutional," they immediately think nursing home and cringe. But institutional care for the aging doesn't necessarily have to be provided in a nursing home. Also on the list are assisted living centers, adult day care facilities, continuing care retirement communities, congregate apartments; the list goes on and on.

Not every option is available in every community. Almost all communities will have nursing homes; many will have assisted living centers. Few will have continuing care retirement communities. For that reason, you need to contact the Area Agency on Aging where your parents live—a number you should clearly have on speed dial at this point. The people there can outline the list of available local institutional options and help you understand the scope of each one.

I'll briefly define a few of these so you can get a sense of what's out there and what might fit your parent's need when the time comes.

Nursing Homes

Nursing homes are residential facilities where Mom/Dad live permanently or on a short-stay basis while recuperating from an illness or medical procedure. Nursing homes provide twenty-four-hour care and supervision by licensed nurses, and they are generally for seniors largely incapable of providing for their basic needs—the "activities of daily living" from early in this chapter.

Nursing homes emphasize "medical care," with the facility coordinating everything from medications to various types of therapies. They also provide for the soft services like mealtime assistance and help toileting, bathing, dressing, and grooming. Most offer some form of religious services for those who wish to partake.

You should also know that nursing homes must be licensed. That's good; it means records exist that you can examine to determine the quality of care offered by a particular nursing home. And you definitely should examine those records. In most states, the department of health (it will go by various names in each state) is the place to start your search for the records. If you shop around for a car or a refrigerator, then you should clearly be shopping around for the best care you can find for your parent.

Assisted Living Centers

Residential facilities are much like small apartment complexes. These are designed largely for aging in place for seniors who don't need the total care provided by a nursing home, but who don't want to or can't live entirely on their own. As such, they're designed to maintain a certain level of independence.

Assisted living centers provide round-the-clock staffing, and generally have apartment-style rooms wrapping around common areas including a common dining room. The center typically provides meals and whatever personal assistance might be required, and the apartments typically provide a bath and a kitchenette, both of which might be on a shared basis in some centers. Nurses are on staff to manage medical and health care needs.

If you're considering an assisted living center, be aware that some are private centers—meaning they generally accept only private pay residents—while others accept Medicaid. Assisted living centers are also typically licensed, so you can do the requisite homework to check up on the centers you might be interested in.

Congregate Apartments

Congregate apartments are multiunit housing of various kinds designed for seniors who can manage their own affairs or are at least semi-independent. These function similarly to assisted living centers in that they provide common areas and a common dining area, while the living units provide a room that doubles as living room and bedroom, a bathroom, and a kitchenette. Not all provide three meals a day, though they do offer at least one meal. Individual services, like cleaning, transportation, and personal assistance are not always included in the monthly cost, but are billed separately, per service.

A key difference: On-site medical and/or health care generally isn't commonplace, though personal care services are typically provided. As such, congregate care isn't an option for parents who have health needs that require routine or daily care because they are taking medication.

Moreover, these facilities are not always licensed or regulated by states, so you'll need to check on that in your parent's particular state if this arrangement appeals to you and your parent. If the center you're researching doesn't require licensing, then you'll need to do some word-of-mouth homework to find families who have experiences they're willing to share.

Continuing Care Retirement Communities

Think of a condominium complex wrapped around a nursing home and you pretty much have the correct mental image of what are known as CCRCs. In some cases, you might want to picture a high-end cruise ship with a nursing home in the middle; these facilities can be exceedingly exclusive.

CCRCs operate on a so-called continuum-of-care model, in which seniors move into a condo while they're fully capable of managing their own lives. And then, as they age and various health and medical needs begin to arise, they transition into an assisted living arrangement, often remaining in their own condo, and then into the on-site nursing home if necessary. At that point, the person moves out of the condo permanently.

The biggest issue with CCRCs is that a senior who already needs the kind of care provided by an assisted living center or nursing home cannot move into one. These are solely for folks who can still get around on their own. Indeed, in some cases you have people moving into these who are still working, often as doctors or lawyers or such. CCRCs typically require the oldest spouse be at least sixty-two years old to move in, though the other spouse can be younger.

CCRCs are very expensive, generally starting near $100,000 and moving into the low millions. Residents also pay a monthly fee that ranges between $1,500 and $3,000 that covers everything from maintenance and dog walking to gourmet meals and laundry service. The properties operate like real estate, with a twist. Mom/Dad—or their offspring—buy a unit in a CCRC complex and then, when Mom/Dad dies or moves into the nursing home, the unit is sold. The way many CCRC rules work is that the owner of the unit gets back 100% of the original cost, and then the CCRC and the owner split the profits from the sale in some pre-established fashion.

The big benefit: the health care kicker. Along with the various services, the monthly fees also entitle a resident to between thirty days and up to six months of assisted living or skilled nursing care at no added costs. After that, residents must pay a monthly fee for the care, which can range from about $100 a day to roughly $5,000 a month. At that point, however, the resident typically sells the condo and effectively trades the monthly condo fees for the monthly health care costs. Moreover, those monthly health care costs are typically much less than the costs of similar facilities in a given community.

If Mom/Dad has a large enough bankroll, or if you have a large enough bankroll and you see the benefits of a CCRC, these can be a very effective way to care for parents. The price of condos tends to rise over time, since demand in the senior housing market doesn't fluctuate to the same degree as it does in the traditional real estate market. The ability to transition seamlessly from condo to assisted living to nursing home is a strong selling point. Still, this option is entirely a matter of costs, because it's so expensive.

Who it's best for: It depends on the type of institution you're talking about. Nursing homes and assisted living centers are for those retirees who can no longer manage their own affairs and need specialized care that isn't feasible in a home setting. In other words, if Mom/Dad has Alzheimer's or they need care for more than just a few hours a day, an institutional arrangement is probably best. Assisted living is best for aging parents not able to live independently, but who don't need the higher level of care provided in a nursing home. Nursing homes, meanwhile, tend to be those who need near round-the-clock care and assistance.

A congregate apartment setting best fits the needs of a senior who is at least semi-independent but needs some assistance in some areas. It's a toss-up, though, between a congregate apartment and remaining at home and relying on in-home care services. In this situation you have to run a cost-benefit analysis to determine which arrangement makes the most sense financially, based on the kinds of services Mom/Dad needs.

And a CCRC is clearly for a senior who is 100% mobile—and might even still be working—but planning ahead for the day when assisted living or nursing home needs arise. This option is also a function of age, medical condition, and the size of the assets available. And because the expense is so high, it's obviously an option for a limited number of people.

The Benefits and Drawbacks of Institutional Care

The Benefits of Institutional Care

The clear benefit of institutional care is the care itself and the peace of mind you have in knowing that someone is looking out for Mom/Dad continually. This is round-the-clock care in most cases, erasing from your mind worries about a parent home alone during those hours when you or a sitter or other professional aren't around.

- *Specialized care:* Institutions offer special units specifically designed for Alzheimer's or other mental disorders that generally cannot be delivered cost-effectively at home. These are also secured settings that keep Alzheimer's patients from wandering off the property and getting hurt.
- *Social activities*: As I noted earlier in this book, socialization has a big impact on an elderly person's health and mental state. Nursing homes and assisted living centers can better deal with the isolation issues that otherwise

impact a parent living alone. The facilities sponsor all manner of social activities, from card games to cinema nights to outings that keep seniors active in their communities. That benefits Mom/Dad's mental health.

• *Peace of mind*: I've mentioned this benefit previously, but it applies again here. When you feel comfortable that Mom/Dad is appropriately cared for, and when that burden is no longer on your shoulders, you can return to a more normal life.

The Drawbacks of Institutional Care

There are two drawbacks of institutional care—and they're both potentially significant.

1. *Guilt:* Many people worry about whether they did the right thing by sticking a parent in a nursing home or assisted living center, particularly when Mom/Dad expressed through the years a clear wish to remain at home until death. Even when you know in your heart that an institutional setting is the only right answer, that still doesn't negate feelings that you've somehow betrayed your parents. After all, you are taking away their independence, and that can be a huge mental blow to a parent.

   Quality of care also hits the guilt realm. Many nursing homes across the country have been dinged for lack of cleanliness, subpar food, lax care, distribution of wrong medications, and patients who are left alone for too long. Some nursing homes have had Alzheimer's patients walk out of facilities and get lost. This isn't widespread, mind you, but it does happen, and it raises quality of care questions that can nag at you.

2. *The costs*: Institutional care is a pricey proposition, no two ways about it. What you want to provide to your parent, or what Mom/Dad might hope to afford, might be well out of the realm of reality simply because the services are so expensive.

As such, this is an area where you really need to shop around, because prices can vary widely. Too many options exist to detail each one separately in these pages, but here's a look at the prices for several options, as of mid-2010:

The Costs of Institutional Care

Nursing homes: The average rate for nursing homes in America was $219 a day for a private room according to MetLife, which surveys these costs annually. That's nearly $80,000 a year. A semiprivate room costs $198 a day, or more than $72,000 yearly. For that fee, Mom/Dad typically receives room and board, nursing care, medication management, and assistance with the activities of daily living and such.

To be sure, those costs span a wide spectrum, depending on geography and the type of nursing home you're looking at. Rates in Alaska were as much as $618 a day, while in Louisiana costs were as low as $121 a day. Medicaid patients don't face these costs, since Medicaid pays the bills of nursing home care. However, not all nursing homes accept Medicaid. The facilities that do

accept Medicaid tend to be lower caliber and more institutional in appearance and care than what you'll find
in a private pay nursing home. That's not to imply they
provide substandard care. It's simply to note that it is
what it is, and if you or your parent cannot afford private
pay, a Medicaid facility might be the only option.

Assisted living centers: On an average basis, assisted
living centers cost about $3,100 a month, or more than
$37,000 a year.

Again, though, the range is vast and depends on
whether you're talking about a studio, one-bedroom, or
two-bedroom apartment unit, and whether the unit has a
private bath or shared bath. The lowest rates at the time
I wrote this were down near $2,000 a month; the high-
est exceeded $5,200.

These are "base rates," and what goes into the base
can vary by facility. Typically, base rates cover care
and monitoring, help with the activities of daily living,
housekeeping/laundry, recreational opportunities, transportation when necessary, and two or more meals per
day. Additional services Mom/Dad might require come
off an à la carte menu, and that will impact the overall
monthly price.

When shopping around, make sure you're comparing
apples to apples in terms of what the base rate covers,
and what the added costs are for the services your parent might need. You might find that a facility with a
slightly higher base rate is actually the most affordable
because it covers more of the services Mom/Dad needs,
limiting the number of à la carte services you have to
pay for separately.

Continuing care retirement communities: We covered some of this several pages back when explaining what these are. CCRCs are very expensive and generally well outside the options of most families.

The cost of buying access to a CCRC starts at nearly $100,000 and, depending on the unit and the geography, can top out up near about $2.5 million. On top of that are monthly fees that range from about $1,500 to roughly $3,000.

If you or your parents can afford the hefty outlay up front, then a CCRC might make sense, because the monthly fees are comparable to an assisted living center and can be sharply less than a nursing home. If Mom/Dad cannot afford a unit, maybe you can. In one of the small but growing trends in this area of eldercare, adult children are buying CCRC units for parents who are still healthy enough to move in. Doing so addresses all sorts of issues. You're getting your parent into a very nice complex where there are so many activities that the joke is that seniors move into CCRCs to die of exhaustion. Mom/Dad has guaranteed access to various levels of care as those needs arise, all without leaving home. The transition between home and nursing care is seamless. And at the end, you have an asset you can sell to recoup your money and, potentially, a profit.

But, again, this is only for seniors who are at least sixty-two years old and who have no medical issues that already require assisted living or nursing home care.

Who pays: It all depends on the type of facility Mom/Dad is going into, and your parent's financial condition—or yours. Medicare will pay some limited costs of nursing home care, but generally only after a "qualifying hospital stay" of typically three days or more. Medicare generally does not pay for assisted living, since it is considered a form of long-term care, or custodial care, not all of which is medically necessary. The only assisted living costs Medicare covers are short-term rehabilitation costs when a patient is recovering from an illness, injury, or surgery. Medicare does not pay for places like CCRCs.

Medicaid will pay most nursing home costs, but only for people with limited income and assets—and limited basically means impoverished. And Medicaid will pay only at facilities certified by the government, so that means not every nursing home is on the list. Some nursing homes do not seek certification because they don't cater to Medicaid patients. Medicaid will pay for some assisted living services, since the costs can be cheaper on the system than are nursing homes. But you need to check with the state Medicaid offices where your parents live to determine eligibility in that state. And you have to hope there is an assisted living center nearby that accepts Medicaid, since not all do. Medicaid is a nonissue with CCRCs since people who can afford to move into one are clearly not eligible for Medicaid.

Long-term care policies widely cover nursing home and assisted living center costs, but before your parent invests in a policy make sure you understand exactly what is and is not covered.

A final option for payment is personal resources. An estimated half of all people in nursing homes are paying the costs from their own savings. After that money is gone, these folks often end up on Medicaid, since they've drained their available resources and, thus, become impoverished in the eyes of the Medicaid system. Private pay is also big among assisted living center residents.

Ultimately, no single housing arrangement is perfect for every family, and even the one you and your parent settle on will have its flaws. The goal, though, isn't to find the absolute perfect arrangement, but to find one that addresses the key issues your family has in the most affordable manner you can.

Finally, you must include Mom/Dad in the decision, to the degree your parent is mentally capable of participating in the discussion. As well, you must include any siblings you have. You want everyone who has an emotional tie to this decision involved in the process so that everyone can express concerns, and that those concerns can be addressed effectively and all participants are on board.

I know the process is challenging. I saw this in my own family's life as my mother-in-law and her siblings struggled with caring for their aging father, the patriarch of a very close family. I watched through the years as my mother-in-law handled many of his affairs, as the family hired an in-home caregiver to help manage his daily needs, and as the family ultimately came to the tough conclusion that it was time for Dad to live out his life in a nursing home. Each step was harder than the last. But the stresses on the family were growing increasingly more challenging with each passing year, as were the expanding medical needs.

Institutional care, though an emotional minefield early on, provided the respite and the peace of mind the brothers and sisters needed. Tough as it was mentally, the family knew they'd made the right decisions along the way.

So if you do find yourself in a situation where you are considering institutional care for Mom/Dad, don't lose yourself in loathing and guilt. Open yourself to the possibility that just maybe you're doing something right for your parent and for yourself.

6

The Health

HERE'S TO YOUR MENTAL health. You're going to need all the encouragement you can muster when dealing with the litany of doctors, medical bills, insurance, and the Medicare/Medicaid systems that will swirl around Mom/Dad at some point.

For several years I watched my mother-in-law deal with all of this with her father, then in his nineties. She would stop by from time to time just ranting about all the red tape she had to deal with for him, all the insurance claims submissions, all the doctor's visits and hospital procedures billed improperly, all the—well, all the *everything.* In short, helping manage a parent's health care necessities can be a real pain.

Some of this chapter will seem repetitive. That's a function of the span of health issues; they touch on everything from money to housing to documents—and even The Talk. After all, you have to talk to your parents about the health matters that currently exist as well as their desires related to health issues that will arise in the future.

This chapter, though, will expand on health topics briefly touched on elsewhere. Our topics are confined to just two: the Medicare/Medicaid system and long-term care insurance.

Medicare/Medicaid will apply to the vast majority of retirees. Long-term care won't, because of its expense and the exclusive nature of the underwriting.

Before beginning with Medicare/Medicaid, I encourage you to talk to the local Medicare/Medicaid office where your parent lives. I know I've written that many times, but it's crucial to understand that I don't expect anyone to become an expert on the Byzantine Medicare/Medicaid system, and I'm certainly not an expert on all the nuances that can exist. The reason I frequently encourage you to reach out to the agencies is because it's that important to understand the rules by which your parent must play. Indeed, those rules change for these systems from time to time, and you want to be sure you're working with the most up-to-date information before making any elections or health care decisions. To locate the Medicaid office in your parent's state, go to the website for the National Association of State Medicaid Directors (www.nasmd.org) and search for "Links." You'll find an interactive map on that page that will link you directly to the appropriate website in the appropriate state.

Medicare/Medicaid

COMBINED, THESE TWO GOVERNMENT-SPONSORED programs cover the bulk of retirees. But the two programs are vastly different from one another.

Which one your parent falls into—and, thus, which part of this chapter you should care about—depends on one question: Are your parents categorized as "low income"?

If so, then you want to read about Medicare and Medicaid, since eligible parents can enroll in both. If not, then you can just stick to the Medicare section, since Medicaid is a nonissue.

Before diving into the guts of each, let's look at the two programs side by side, so you get a broad feel with each. Note: The data in the chart below are as of 2010.

Comparing Medicare and Medicaid		
	Medicare	**Medicaid**
Eligibility	Age based: All people sixty-five or older are eligibile; some younger people are eligible, based on disability or certain conditions. * Note: Dual eligibility is possible for low-income people over the age of sixty-five.	Income based; all ages eligible for low-income people.
Administration	A program administered by the federal government, meaning policies and rules are identical from one state to another.	A state-run program, meaning rules and policies can and do vary by state.
Finding information locally	Medicare information is available from local Social Security offices.	Medicaid information is available from county, parish, social-services, and welfare offices.

	Medicare	Medicaid
Comparing Medicare and Medicaid (continued)		
Coverage	Generally covers doctor, hospital, and lab fees; outpatient procedures; equipment and supplies; home health care; physical therapy; and prescription drugs. But all of that depends on whether coverage comes from Medicare part A, B, C, or D.	Generally covers what Medicare covers, plus what Medicare doesn't, such as long-term care needs.
Cost	Depends on various factors. **Part A:** Costs up to $461/month, depending on work history, as recorded by the Social Security Administration. **Part B:** Optional. Costs range from $96.40 to $308.30/month, depending on income level. **Part C:** Costs vary widely. But must have Medicare parts A & B to qualify.	Requires no premiums or deductibles, and medical services providers may not charge patients for costs that exceed the amount Medicaid pays to the provider. Some states may charge a nominal deductible or other form of cost sharing for certain services.
	Part D: Costs vary widely, based on the chosen prescription plan, but there are three costs: monthly premium, annual deductible, and co-pay. Average monthly premium is $30.36. The standard annual deductible is $295, though that varies. Co-pay varies as well, based on the chosen plan.	

Medicare

At its core, Medicare is a government-sponsored health insurance program. Workers fund the bulk of the costs of coverage through a Medicare tax levied on income, while Medicare recipients pay some costs through fees and deductibles for certain Medicare options.

Medicare coverage is available to people over the age of sixty-five, regardless of income—though that could change in the future. Medicare is a financially troubled program and congressional leaders for years have sought ways to guarantee continuing coverage, while at the same time reining in some of the ballooning medical costs. That means Congress at some point could impose "means testing," which could limit eligibility or require wealthier retirees to pay a larger portion of their medical costs, or some combination of those two.

As of this writing, Medicare is built in four parts: A, B, C, and D. The best way to understand the program is to understand what each part covers, what the insurance doesn't cover, and what each part costs.

Part A: Hospital Insurance

What it covers: Inpatient hospital care, including critical care, inpatient rehabilitation facilities, and long-term care hospitals. It also covers hospice and home health services, as well as skilled nursing facilities, such as a temporary stay in a nursing home after a hospitalization or an injury.

Hospital charges covered are for semiprivate rooms (unless

a private room is "medically necessary"). The program also covers meals, general nursing needs, and drugs prescribed as part of the inpatient treatment plan. Medicare will *not* cover items such as televisions or telephones, if a hospital charges for those separately. Nor will it cover personal items like a toothbrush, razor, slippers, etc.

Medicare's skilled nursing coverage (i.e., care provided in an assisted living center or nursing home) also limits payments to a semiprivate room and meals, as well as skilled nursing and rehab services that are necessary. To qualify, though, Mom/Dad must move into that facility—*on a temporary basis only*—for care related directly to a hospitalization that lasted three days or longer. The doctor must order the care.

Medicare does *not* cover long-term care or custodial care in a nursing home or assisted living center.

In terms of home health services, Medicare only pays for medically necessary services. A doctor must order the service, it must be provided by a Medicare-certified agency, and Mom/Dad must be homebound, meaning that leaving home requires a major effort. Additionally, as noted in the paragraph immediately above, this must be part-time or intermittent skilled nursing care, not long-term custodial care. Home health can include physical or occupational therapy and speech-language pathology. Services can include durable medical equipment and medical supplies for use at home. (For more details, see the section in the previous chapter on in-home services and Medicare.)

How to enroll: The Social Security Administration administers the Medicare program, and people age sixty-five are automatically enrolled when they sign up to receive Social

Security payments. The Medicare card arrives about three months prior to the sixty-fifth birthday.

Those who do not receive Social Security at sixty-five must sign up for Part A through the local Social Security office. This should be done three months before the sixty-fifth birthday.

TIP: For people not eligible for premium-free Medicare benefits, pay close attention to the Medicare enrollment window. Medicare provides a seven-month window to enroll in Part A. The window opens three months prior to the month of the sixty-fifth birthday, and ends three months after the sixty-fifth birthday month. In other words, if Mom/Dad turns sixty-five on July 17, then enrollment opens in April (three months before July), and then closes at the end of October. Seven months. If Mom/Dad do not enroll when first eligible, then Medicare increases the monthly costs by 10% for double the amount of time that coverage wasn't purchased. In other words, if Mom/Dad enroll two years after eligibility began, the 10% penalty applies for four years.

What it costs: Typically, people do not pay a premium for Part A because they or a spouse paid the premiums through those Medicare payroll tax deductions during their working years. A parent needs forty quarters, or ten years, of paying into the system to be fully covered.

Some people, however, do pay. If one or both of your parents worked and paid into the Medicare system for less than ten years, a monthly fee is assessed for as much as $461. How much Mom/Dad must pay depends on how many years your parent paid into the system.

For 2010, the Part A premium is $254 a month for people who have between thirty and thirty-nine quarters of paying into the Medicare system. The monthly premium jumps to $461 for people with less than thirty quarters.

Deductibles: Part A imposes deductibles that Mom/Dad must pay. The deductibles vary, depending on the length of time spent in the hospital or skilled nursing facility. The deductibles are based on each "benefit period" (see the definition below). Medicare pays all covered costs after your parent meets the deductible. For each benefit period, Mom/Dad pay these amounts below, based on 2010 rules:

- A total of $1,100 for a hospital stay of between 1 and 60 days.
- Coinsurance of $275 per day for days 61 through 90 of a hospital stay.
- Coinsurance of $550 per day for days 91 through 150 of a hospital stay. These count toward lifetime reserve days (see the definition below).
- All costs for each day beyond day 150.
- For skilled nursing care, coinsurance of $137.50 a day for days 21 through 100 in a skilled nursing facility.

Benefit period: A benefit period begins on the day Mom/Dad enters the hospital or skilled nursing facility, and it ends when your parent has received no hospital or skilled nursing care for sixty consecutive days after discharge. If Mom/Dad reenters the hospital or skilled nursing facility on day sixty-one or after, a new benefit period begins, and your parent must pay the deductible for each benefit period. There's no limit to the number of benefit periods Mom/Dad can have.

Lifetime reserve days: Medicare provides sixty extra days of coverage when Mom/Dad is in the hospital for more than ninety days during a single benefit period. These sixty reserve days are a one-and-done benefit, meaning that once they're used up, they are never replenished.

During these reserve days, Medicare pays all covered costs except for a daily coinsurance amount that your parent must pay. Medigap policies, assuming your parent has one, often cover this coinsurance cost, and they generally include an additional 365 lifetime reserve days.

In practice, these reserve days mean, for instance, that if Mom/Dad is in the hospital for, say, ninety-five days, five days could fall under lifetime reserve days. Of course Mom/Dad can choose not to use reserve days if that makes sense for some reason.

When would it make sense not to use reserve days? Well, if the hospital costs are the same or marginally higher than the coinsurance of $550/day in 2010, then it can make sense to keep the days for later in life when a hospital stay might be more expensive. Or, if the daily cost of the hospital is less than the coinsurance, then there's little reason to consume reserve days.

Part B: Medical Insurance

What it covers: Part B provides coverage for medically necessary services, ranging from doctor visits to outpatient care to home health sevices. It also covers some preventive services, and medical services that Part A misses, such as physical and occupational therapies.

How to enroll: Most retirees are automatically signed up for Part B when they enroll in Part A. Mom/Dad can opt out of Part B if they can't afford it or if they already pay for private insurance or have health coverage through a corporate retiree benefit plan.

If your parent is already covered by Medicare and you want to know if Part B is included in the coverage, look at Mom/Dad's Medicare card; it will show which Medicare parts your parent is enrolled in.

TIP: If Mom/Dad rely on Medicare Part B, make sure any doctors they need to see "accept assignment" before making an appointment.

Medicare dictates what it will pay for various medical services, known as the Medicare-approved amount. A doctor who accepts assignment agrees to accept as full payment whatever fee Medicare pays for the service he's rendering. That means no additional charge to Mom/Dad. A doctor who does not accept assignment can charge Mom/Dad for the costs that Medicare doesn't pick up.

What it costs: Even if Mom/Dad has forty quarters or ten years paying into the Medicare system, the program charges a monthly premium for Part B coverage. The premium typically comes out of your parent's Social Security paycheck.

If you're helping your parent determine the Medicare

coverage that makes the most sense, examine the chart below to determine what Part B will cost on a monthly basis as of 2010. The income figures are based on so-called **modified gross income**. You can determine that by looking at your parent's tax return (when determining income levels, Medicare looks at returns from the previous two years). Take the adjusted gross income (line 37 on IRS form 1040), and add to that any tax-exempt interest income (line 8b). That's modified gross income.

Also, be aware that Part B deductibles and premiums can change each January, so the fee your parent initially pays isn't necessarily the fee that will prevail continually.

Part B Monthly Premiums		
If your income in 2008 was		
File individual tax return	File joint tax return	The cost is
$85,000 or below	$170,000 or below	$110.50 *
$85,001–$107,000	$170,001–$214,000	$154.70
$107,001–$160,000	$214,001–$320,000	$221.00
$160,001–$214,000	$320,001–$428,000	$287.30
above $214,000	above $428,000	$353.60
* For 2010, most people will pay the 2009 rate of $96.40/month		

Along with premiums, Medicare Part B also imposes a yearly deductible of $155. That means Mom/Dad are responsible for the first $155 in medical costs that Part B would otherwise cover. After that Part B kicks in and pays 80% of the Medicare-approved amount for the medical service rendered. Mom/Dad must cover the other 20% or rely on private insurance or a Medigap policy (more on Medigap in a moment).

Part B is voluntary coverage. If a parent cannot afford the coverage, then there's no need to buy it. However, as with Part A, a parent who doesn't sign up for Part B when first eligible but decides later to purchase coverage faces a penalty. (Parents sign up for Parts A and B concurrently.)

If Mom/Dad wants to opt out of Part B because the cost is too dear, look into the Medicare Savings Program in your parent's state. This program helps people with limited income pay some or all of their Medicare premiums, and in some cases will pay necessary deductibles and co-pays for Parts A and B. To qualify, a parent must meet the following conditions:

- Enroll in Part A.
- If single: Your parent must earn a monthly income of less than $1,239 and have resources of less than $8,100.
- If married and living together: They must earn a monthly income of less than $1,660 and have resources of less than $12,910.

To find the local contact where your parent lives, go to www.medicare.gov and then search "Medicare Savings Program." A link will pop up that lists all the state contacts.

Part C: Medicare Advantage Plan

What it is: Part C is effectively an HMO-like option that combines Parts A and B into a single plan. The primary difference is that private insurers approved by Medicare provide the coverage.

In many cases, Part C coverage is less costly for retirees, and plan providers often sweeten coverage by including additional benefits as well as prescription drug coverage, known as Part D (which we will get to next). Moreover, electing to buy Part C coverage means there's no need to pay for a Medigap policy.

The potential downside is that Part C typically makes patients stay within a prescribed network of doctors and hospitals. That differs from Parts A and B, both of which allow freedom of choice.

These Medicare Advantage plans come in various flavors, including the following:

- *Medicare Preferred Provider Organization (PPO):* Allows Mom/Dad to see any doctor or specialist; however, if that provider is not within the network, out-of-pocket costs go up. Typically no referral is needed to see a specialist.

- *Medicare Health Maintenance Organization (HMO):* Allows Mom/Dad to visit doctors in the HMO network only. Typically a referral is required to see a specialist.

- *Medicare Private Fee-for-Service (PFFS):* Allows Mom/Dad to see any doctor or specialist, so long as that provider accepts the program's fees and conditions. A referral is not required to see a specialist.

- *Medicare Medical Savings Account (MSA):* These plans have two parts:

    1. *A high-deductible health insurance plan* for which coverage doesn't kick in until Mom/Dad meets a high annual deductible. The size of the deductible varies by plan.

2. *A savings account* into which Medicare deposits money each year that Mom/Dad can use to pay health costs before meeting the deductible. The money is held at a bank the plan selects, and that cash—as well as any interest it generates—isn't subject to income taxes so long as it's used for health care costs. If Mom/Dad spends all the money in the account yet still has medical costs, then your parent must cover those costs until the health plan deductible is met. During that period, doctors or other health care providers cannot charge more than the Medicare-approved amount. After meeting the deductible, the health plan takes over and begins to pick up the additional costs. Any money remaining in the account at the end of a given year stays in the account and can be used for future health care costs.

How to enroll: Numerous insurers offer Part C coverage, but not every insurer covers every corner of the country. As such, contact the Social Security Administration where your parent lives and request information on the insurers in that area that provide Medicare Part C coverage.

What it costs: Again, the possibilities are all over the map. Some charge no premium, though Mom/Dad must still pay for Part B coverage. Others do charge a premium, though it is often cheaper than buying Part B and/or Medigap coverage.

Though Part C is often cheaper, always do your homework when helping your parent choose Medicare coverage. Part C avoids the premiums and deductibles incurred with

Parts A and B, but Part C typically has its own premiums, deductibles, and co-pays. You want to do an apples-to-apples comparison, or have an eldercare attorney or financial planner help you with the comparison, to ensure that you and your parents are choosing the plan that makes the most sense financially.

Part D: Prescription Drug Coverage

What it is: Part D provides insurance coverage for doctor-prescribed pharmaceuticals, and it is of particular benefit for retirees dependent on very expensive drugs that can consume a large portion of a monthly paycheck.

Part D pays for both branded and generic prescriptions filled by participating pharmacies. As with Part C, Part D plans are run by private companies. As such, each plan can vary in terms of the drugs covered.

Before signing up with any prescription plan, make sure that plan covers any drugs—particularly the most expensive drugs—that Mom/Dad currently buy. And make sure the plan covers specific drugs in the quantity or dose your parent requires. Also make sure that the plan your parent is considering works with local pharmacies your parent uses.

How to enroll: To get Part D, your parent must already have Part A and/or Part B. Those parents can enroll in a separate prescription drug plan. But because there are so many different Part D plans on offer, Mom and Dad have to figure out which plan best meets their needs and then contact that provider to determine how to enroll.

A parent who enrolls in Part C (Medicare Advantage)

typically has prescription drug coverage as part of that plan.

TIP: Even if Mom/Dad are not taking many prescription drugs when you first get involved with helping them, don't reflexively disregard the need for Part D coverage. As people age, medical problems increase, which increases the need for medications. Having Part D coverage is insurance against potentially large pharmacy bills in future years.

What it costs: Part D plans impose a monthly premium, a yearly deductible, and a co-pay (or coinsurance) for each prescription filled. This applies to those who buy Part D coverage separately, since drugs are covered by Part C plans, which have their own deductibles and premiums.

Because private companies run prescription drug plans, and because the various plans cover different drugs, Part D plans vary widely in terms of costs. In general, the plans that cover the largest number of drugs, and those that cover the most expensive medications charge the biggest premiums.

On average, Part D plans cost about $32 a month, but, again, that varies widely depending on the plan and its coverage.

In 2010, the standard annual deductible was about $310, though that varies too. (So many variables exist with Medicare that it's impossible not to throw around caveats and generalities.)

The big—big—caveat to remember with Part D is that once drug costs in a single year reach a certain level, about $2,830, Medicare stops paying for prescriptions, leaving your parent to pick up the cost. Coverage kicks in again once drug costs reach a second level—$4,550 in 2010. At that level, Medicare will pay about 95% of drug costs for the rest of the year.

This hole between $2,830 and $4,550 is known as the "doughnut hole." It won't be an issue for parents who don't rely on expensive medications. But for others on pricey drugs, it will be an issue you must take into consideration.

Finally, for people with low incomes and limited assets, Medicare provides what it calls "extra help" in paying premiums, deductibles, and co-pays. Mom/Dad must first be enrolled in a Medicare Prescription Drug plan to obtain this help. Moreover, these plans generally do not have a coverage gap, that doughnut hole.

Certain people automatically qualify for financial assistance in paying for Part D coverage: those who are "dual eligible" for Medicare and Medicaid, those who receive help from Medicaid in paying for Medicare Part B premiums, or those who receive Supplemental Security Income.

Others may qualify for help in paying for Part D coverage based on these financial criteria for 2010:

Medicare Part D Financial Criteria

	Single	Married
Income	$16,245	$21,855
Assets *	$12,510	$25,010

* Excludes home and car

For more information or to apply for help for a parent, contact the Social Security Administration.

Medigap: Supplemental Insurance

What it is: Medigap is a health insurance policy sold by a private company that fills the coverage gaps in Parts A and B. Generally your parent must have Parts A and B to buy a Medigap policy.

These policies are person specific, meaning you can't buy one policy to cover both parents. Each parent must have an individual policy.

The challenge with Medigap comes in choosing which policy to buy, since ten versions are available—Plans A through N. (Plans E, H, I, and J were eliminated in 2010, although consumers who previously had any of those four plans can continue to keep them, and the benefits will not change.) Not all plans are available in all areas of the country.

Each plan has a different set of basic and extended benefits. The plans, however, are standardized, meaning every Plan G looks like every other Plan G, though cost can differ from one insurer to the next.

All Medigap plans include the following coverage:

- hospital coinsurance
- 365 additional days of full hospital coverage beyond what Medicare provides
- full or partial coverage of the 20% coinsurance for doctor charges and other Plan B covered services

- full or partial coverage each year for the first three pints of blood needed
- full or partial coverage of hospice coinsurance for drugs and respite care

Depending on which Medigap policy your parent chooses, the policies can include coverage for:

- hospital deductibles
- skilled nursing facility coinsurance
- Part B deductibles
- emergency care outside the United States
- at-home recovery
- preventive care that Medicare doesn't cover
- "excess charges," or charges above the Medicare-approved amount charged by doctors who do not participate in the Medicare program

The chart on the following page indicates what each Medigap plan covers.

Medigap

A checkmark in the box means that Medigap plan covers 100% of the benefit. A percentage indicates the plan covers that percentage of the benefit's cost.

Benefit	Medigap Plans									
	A	B	C	D	F	G	K	L	M	N
Part A coinsurance hospital costs up to an additional 365 days after Medicare benefits are used up	✓	✓	✓	✓	✓	✓	✓	✓	✓	✓
Part B coinsurance or co-pay	✓	✓	✓	✓	✓	✓	50%	75%	✓	✓
Blood (first three pints)	✓	✓	✓	✓	✓	✓	50%	75%	✓	✓
Part A hospice care coinsurance/co-pay	✓	✓	✓	✓	✓	✓	50%	75%	✓	✓
Skilled nursing facility coinsurance			✓	✓	✓	✓	50%	75%	✓	✓
Part A deductible		✓	✓	✓	✓	✓	50%	75%	50%	✓
Part B deductible			✓		✓					
Part B excess charges					✓	✓				
Foreign travel emergency (up to plan limits)			✓	✓	✓	✓			✓	✓
Preventive care Part B co-insurance	✓	✓	✓	✓	✓	✓	✓	✓	✓	✓

* After meeting out-of-pocket limits, as well as Part B annual deductible ($155 in 2010), Medigap pays 100% of covered services for the rest of the calendar year.	Out-of-Pocket Limit *	
	$4,620	$2,310

TIP: Medigap polices *do not cover* long-term care, vision or dental care, hearing aids, eyeglasses, or private duty nursing. So don't buy a policy thinking Mom/Dad will be able to rely on that for these expenses.

How to enroll: Mom/Dad have the right to buy a Medigap policy only at certain times, generally during the six-month open enrollment period when they're first eligible to enroll in Medicare. Miss the enrollment window and costs can go up, or insurers can refuse to sell your parent a policy. Some states do have additional open enrollment periods.

For the exact rules in your parent's state, or to find out which Medigap policies are available where your parent lives, contact that state's Department of Insurance or the State Health Insurance Assistance Program, both of which you can Google.

What it costs: With so many different plan options and with so many different insurers selling policies, Medigap prices run the gamut.

Some of the least expensive plans cost less than $100 a month. Some of the most expensive plans can cost $10,000 a year or more. And complicating the calculus is the fact that different insurers offering the same plan can be hundreds or thousands of dollars apart.

As such, Medigap is one area where you really need to do some legwork to make sure you're getting the best deal possible for your parent.

Medicaid

Like Medicare, Medicaid is government-sponsored health coverage. Unlike Medicare, Medicaid is administered by each individual state, though based around certain federal mandates. The upshot is that programs differ in various ways from one state to the next. As such, what you'll read here on Medicaid are the broad basics, since it's impractical in this book to detail all the differences and nuances of each state's plan.

For specific information on the Medicaid system where your parent lives, contact that state's local department of Health and Human Services.

The key factor you need to understand is that Medicaid is a needs-based program. If your parents have assets, there's a pretty good chance they're not going to qualify for Medicaid.

So if your parents have any level of assets (outside of their home and car), you can pretty much skip this section because Medicaid isn't likely to apply. And while you will see/hear/read about Medicaid eligibility strategies, the fact is that's a very tough game to play these days. And a dicey one.

Medicaid has a so-called five-year look-back window that allows the local Medicaid administering agency to look back over an applicant's previous five years of financial transactions. If Medicaid sees a bunch of assets moving around, particularly assets transferred into the names of siblings and offspring, the program can, and will, deny coverage. Moreover, depending on how the transactions were structured, there's a chance that Mom/Dad will no longer have access to the underlying asset, which can really foul up finances going forward. That said, let's dig into Medicaid.

What it is: Medicaid is a federal entitlement program administered by the states, but overseen by the federal Centers for Medicare & Medicaid Services, as well as the U.S. Department of Health and Human Services.

It covered more than 58 million Americans in fiscal year 2007, the latest data at the time of this writing. That represented nearly one in every five Americans. Without Medicaid, the bulk of those people would end up on the rolls of the uninsured.

Medicaid is responsible for $1 of every $6 spent nationally on personal care, and it finances 40%—the largest portion—of the nation's bills for both nursing home and long-term care.

The program covers anyone from children to retirees, and that includes working families. These are people who generally lack access to the private health insurers that cover most Americans. In terms of this book, we're focusing solely on Medicaid's role in providing medical coverage to the elderly.

Nearly two-thirds of all Medicaid recipients, at least as of 2007, were enrolled in a Medicaid Managed Care Program of some sort, either a health maintenance organization (HMO) or through a primary care case management setup (PCCM).

Medicaid recipients are also eligible to receive Medicare, a status known as "dual eligible," as mentioned several pages back. The benefit of dual coverage is that Medicaid often kicks in where Medicare falls short. When it comes to retirees, that's particularly useful for long-term care needs, which Medicare doesn't cover but Medicaid does.

Finally, Medicaid is a so-called entitlement program. That means people who qualify for coverage under their state's guidelines have a federal right to Medicaid coverage *in that state*.

TIP: Just because Mom/Dad qualify for Medicaid in one state doesn't mean that right transfers to another state. Your parent would have to qualify under the new state's guidelines. Thus, if your Medicaid-eligible parent is considering relocating, check to see if they will remain Medicaid eligible in the new location. If not, you might want to reconsider the move or pick a location where eligibility remains in place.

What it covers: Medicaid essentially covers what any private insurer would cover, plus additional services for dental and vision care. It also picks up the tab for transportation, when necessary, and long-term care, as mentioned previously.

Federal law outlines what coverage states *must* provide, and then states are free to add on to that. These services are covered based on so-called **medical necessity**, as determined by each state's program. The list below details the federally mandated services that each state must provide; I've limited the list to those that would apply to a retiree (family-planning services and pediatric services are clearly irrelevant, for instance).

- physicians' services
- hospital services (inpatient/outpatient)
- lab and x-ray services
- federally qualified health center and rural health clinic services
- nursing facility services for individuals twenty-one and older

- home health care for persons eligible for nursing facility services
- transportation services

Certain other services are technically optional, but because of their necessity they routinely are included in basic Medicaid packages. Prescription drugs are the primary example; all states cover them.

Along with prescriptions, the list of commonly offered optional services applicable to retirees includes:

- clinic services
- care provided by other licensed practitioners
- dental services and dentures
- prosthetic devices, eyeglasses, and durable medical equipment
- rehab and other therapies
- case management
- home- and community-based services
- respiratory care services for ventilator-dependent patients
- personal care services
- hospice services

Medicaid also broadly covers long-term care, and is the largest payer for these services in the country. For parents who require round-the-clock care, the program pays nursing home costs. For parents still capable of living independently, the program pays for home health services, as well as personal care, medical equipment, adult day care, case management, and even respite for caregivers, among other expenses.

Now, the caveat in all of this is that except for children

(and they're not germane to this book) individual state programs can place limits on covered services. They can, for instance, limit the number of physician visits your parent can accumulate or cap the prescription drugs that are covered. Moreover, each state can define "medically necessary" differently, meaning a procedure covered in one state as medically necessary might not be covered in another state.

To get a clear understanding of exactly what Medicaid covers in the state where Mom/Dad lives, contact the local department of health.

How to enroll: To qualify for Medicaid, Mom/Dad must fall within certain financial criteria and belong to one of the groups that are "categorically eligible" to participate in the program. The categories are broad, but specifically they include elderly who receive Supplemental Security Income (SSI).

States can expand coverage to optional groups as well. Among that list are three categories of potential interest when it comes to Mom/Dad:

- Elderly who earn up to 100% of the federally defined poverty level. For 2010, the federal poverty level was annual income of $10,830 for a family of one, and $14,570 for a couple. As such, if a single parent earns less than that in a year, that parent is eligible for Medicaid.
- Elderly residing in nursing facilities with income below 300% of the SSI standard. In 2010, SSI monthly income limits for individuals and couples receiving unearned income were $865 and $1,427.20 respectively. That means if Mom/Dad is in a nursing home, they're eligible

for Medicaid with monthly income below $2,595 for an individual and $4,281.60 as a couple.

- "Medically needy" people who have health care expenses that are high relative to income.

To physically enroll Mom/Dad in Medicaid, head to the local department of health in the city where your parent lives and request a Medicaid application. You will probably have to fill it out in the office. You will need the following documents:

- parent's birth certificate
- parent's driver's license, if Mom/Dad still drives
- parent's Social Security card
- proof of your parent's address
- proof of your parent's insurance, if any
- bank account and any other financial data
- proof of current income, meaning the most recent tax return

The Look-Back Period

Several pages back I mentioned the so-called look-back period. This is a rule Medicaid imposes before granting eligibility to an applicant. The aim of the look-back period is to prevent an otherwise financially capable elderly person from giving away property and assets simply to begin receiving Medicaid immediately. The rule is particularly aimed at those people who try to look impoverished just before they require expensive institutional care at a nursing home.

The look back is a five-year period of time during which Medicaid scrutinizes an applicant's financial history to determine if assets were given away at below fair market prices in order to make the applicant appear poor and, thus, eligible for Medicaid. The period begins upon applying for Medicaid, meaning five years prior to the date of application are under review.

Medicaid will question a transfer that occurs during that look-back period. If the transaction fails, meaning if Medicaid determines it was conducted simply for eligibility reasons, then Medicaid will impose a penalty (more on that in a moment).

Not all transactions within the five-year window affect Medicaid. Asset transfers that *do not* impact eligibility are:

- those transacted at fair market values

- those clearly conducted for a purpose other than to qualify for Medicaid

- those done for the sole benefit of an institutionalized elder's spouse or permanently disabled or blind child

The penalty Medicaid imposes is a period of ineligibility for Medicaid, proportionate to the value of the assets gifted or given away within the look-back period.

As part of the look-back process, each state has established standards defining the average monthly cost of long-term care. Local Medicaid programs use those standards to determine the period of ineligibility in the event an asset transfer falls afoul of the look-back period. This is what it looks like in practical terms—and remember, each state sets different standards, so I'm making up an example just to illustrate the point:

Assume that Mom/Dad lives in a state where the average monthly cost of long-term care is $7,500. And assume your parent, within five years of applying for Medicaid, gifted you a stock and bond portfolio valued at $75,000. That transfer violates the look-back period and, thus, imposes a penalty on your parent.

The length of the penalty period is determined by dividing the amount of the transfer (less any value received in that transaction) by the average monthly cost of long-term care. So in this example, $75,000 divided by $7,500 gives us ten months. That's the penalty period. In other words, that's how long a parent has to wait for Medicaid benefits to begin once he or she applies.

Medicaid regulations allow for an appeal. Thus, if Mom/Dad had a reason for making a transfer that initially might not be clear to the local Medicaid program, you can appeal the decision on behalf of your parent. When appealing a denial, however, I encourage you to hire legal counsel, preferably an eldercare lawyer intimately familiar with Medicaid rules.

What it costs: Because this is a program aimed at the poor, Medicaid is largely free.

In some states, however, the local Medicaid program charges consumers a small cost for some services. Many states also impose a prescription drug co-pay of a few dollars.

Check with the Medicaid agency in your parent's state to determine what costs, if any, are imposed for what services.

Long-Term Care Insurance

YOU WILL READ A lot of commentary in the popular press regarding the value of long-term care insurance. Some commentators are for it; some think it's too pricey and full of too many potential risks.

I am one of the fans of long-term care, or LTC. In fact, my wife and I at age forty and forty-one, respectively, purchased policies for ourselves from New York Life. (I am not necessarily recommending New York Life. I mention the name because, as you will read in a moment, it offered the best policy in terms of what we happened to be looking for.)

We bought at such a young age for two reasons: (1) As I mentioned in a previous chapter, LTC is essentially a pass/ fail policy, meaning that if you already have certain ailments when you apply, you won't receive coverage; and (2) the policies grow more expensive with age; in our forties we found policies that offered us all the bells and whistles we wanted at a price we considered affordable.

Why we saw a need for long-term care to begin with gets to the heart of this chapter.

We bought because we want assurances that the costs of our eldercare are covered. We want to know that our finances won't be drained if one or both of us requires nursing home care or assisted living. We want to know that we have a source of funding to afford the services we want at the providers we choose, negating the concerns we have about getting stuck inside the Medicaid system. And we want to know that our eldercare costs won't be a financial burden to our children. Thus, for us, long-term care made a lot of sense.

But that doesn't mean it's right for everyone. LTC is real financial commitment. It's some of the priciest insurance around; it has to be, because it is promising to pay for some of the priciest care available—eldercare. Nursing homes, assisted living centers, and home health care costs (we went through those numbers earlier) can run $50,000 to $80,000 a year or more, depending on the services required when eldercare needs finally arise.

For many people, the pass/fail test and/or the cost of the policy means LTC is simply not an option. And if it seems clear your parent is likely to qualify for Medicaid, then there's no point even thinking about LTC. What money Mom/Dad does have should be used for living comforts instead of funneling into an expensive long-term care policy.

But if your parents have a certain level of assets and won't be eligible for Medicaid, then at least talk to them about considering an LTC policy. Not only will it help them afford the costs of aging, but it will also help you. You won't be called upon to fund those costs, nor will you feel guilty about the Medicaid-funded nursing home where Mom/Dad ends up living.

───────── CONSERVATION STARTER ─────────

"Mom/Dad, I was doing a bit of research on long-term care, trying to determine if it might make sense for you as a way to ensure your nonmedical care is covered if you ever reach the point you can't care for yourself anymore. I have some information I'd like to share with you. So when you're interested in talking about this, let me know."

So, let's dive into what you need to know about long-term care.

What it is: In a nutshell, long-term care is insurance against the cost of old age. To many people, LTC is nursing home insurance. And that's essentially what it was back in its early incarnation. Today, however, LTC helps cover the costs of chronic illnesses or disabilities. Beyond the obvious nursing homes and assisted living centers, the range of services that LTC covers spans home health aides, home-delivered meals, adult day care centers, home chore services, respite for caregivers who provide services to Mom/Dad.

In short, long-term care policies help your parents protect themselves against the financial risks of needing long-term care services, either in an institutional setting or at home.

Who needs coverage: That's difficult to say because no one knows what future health care needs will emerge.

Statistically, 14% of people sixty-five and over need some form of long-term care according to the Health Policy Institute at Georgetown University. Among those eighty-five and older the percentage jumps to about half.

When you look at the data by gender, the numbers are

startling. Elderly women, by far, are the biggest consumers of long-term care services. Among people over sixty-five, 69% of those with long-term care needs are women. And among nursing home residents, 72% are women.

Overall, the U.S. Department of Health and Human Services calculates that a sixty-five-year-old faces a 40% chance of entering a nursing home, and that about 10% of the people who enter will stay there for at least five years. Meanwhile, at any given moment, about one in five Americans over the age of eighty-five resides in a nursing home.

The statistics, however, still don't answer the question of who will ultimately need long-term care. Many people will simply never need coverage, and, in hindsight, having bought a policy will have proven a wasted expense.

Instead, the statistics point to the need to have a discussion with your parent. To what degree does Mom/Dad want to be prepared for the possibility that expensive long-term care needs arise? If buying a policy brings peace of mind, even if it ultimately goes unused, then is that really a wasted expense? Only you and your parents can answer that.

If your parent has no assets, then long-term care is irrelevant because (1) they haven't the money to afford the policy, and (2) they'll likely be eligible for Medicaid anyway.

Parents with wealth of about $500,000 or more, excluding the home, generally don't need an LTC policy either. Those parents are effectively self-insured. (Even at that level, though, some people do buy LTC policies because they want to preserve as much of their wealth as they can to pass along to heirs.)

The families for whom LTC typically makes the most sense are those with assets of between $250,000 and $500,000.

That's because an extended need for long-term care can quickly drain the assets, leaving a surviving spouse with few assets to live on, or few assets for heirs. For these parents LTC is a safety net to cover the catastrophic costs of aging and preserve Mom/Dad's limited amount of assets for other needs.

If a parent with between $250,000 and $500,000 in wealth not tied to the home is single, divorced, or widowed, and the offspring clearly have no need for the inheritance, then skipping the LTC policy can make sense; the assets Mom/Dad has accumulated will likely cover most, if not all of the costs—and there's no competing demand for those assets.

What it covers: LTC policies cover the cost of care when a policyholder, regardless of age, can no longer perform the activities of daily living. (See pages 163–65 in chapter 5, "The House," for a definition of those activities.)

The policies typically cover the costs for:

- skilled nursing care or custodial care in a licensed nursing home or some other type of licensed facility;
- home care services such as skilled or nonskilled nursing care, physical therapy, home health aides, homemaker duties (such as cleaning and cooking), and transportation;
- assisted living costs, adult day care, and other community and alternative care; and
- respite care for caregivers, which allows caregivers a regular break from their duties by providing the costs necessary to hire others to come in temporarily and provide care; a wide body of research has shown that respite for caregivers has, among other benefits, improved

family quality of life and increased the caregiver's capacity to manage the stress of providing care.

Insurers will often require a certain period of time pass before coverage kicks in. This is the exclusionary period. For some insurers, the period might be six months; for others it might be two years. It's a way of effectively penalizing policyholders who wait until they need care before buying coverage.

LTC policies also generally place a limit on benefits. And this you and your parents *must* be aware of.

The limit is generally tied to a predetermined number of years or total benefits paid out. Policies generally are built around time frames of two through five years, though some of the priciest policies offer unlimited coverage.

Dollar limits are reached when total benefits paid out reach what the policy promises to pay over its predetermined life. So, for instance, if Mom/Dad has paid for benefits of $100 a day for two years, the policy stops paying once your parent has consumed $73,000 in long-term care costs (365 x 2 x 100)—even if that happens before two years has expired.

If your parent chooses to pay for unlimited coverage, then you'll not have to worry about number of years or amount paid out. But not every insurer offers an unlimited policy, and those that do charge dearly for them because of the risk the insurer is assuming.

When to buy: The earlier the better.

Since we're talking about people who are already retired or are very close to it, I'll skip the discourse on why people in their forties and early fifties are wise to consider it (and they should).

There are two reasons to buy sooner rather than later:

1. LTC policies grow progressively more expensive with age. So, a younger parent will find policies more affordable.
2. And, as I've pointed out a few times, LTC is a pass/fail policy. As such, you want Mom/Dad to look at policies while they're still healthy enough to obtain coverage. That tends to be a younger retiree.

The median age of purchase has been coming down in recent years and is currently in the low sixties.

TIP: If Mom/Dad is buying a policy earlier in retirement, make sure the policy includes inflation protection.

Buying a policy at fifty-five or sixty or even sixty-five means Mom/Dad might not need the coverage for twenty to thirty years. Health care costs in that time can soar. Consider an LTC policy bought twenty years earlier that promised to pay a fixed $100 per day. The daily rate might have easily covered expected expenses at the time of purchase. But consider that policy after the impact of medical cost inflation is factored in.

Apply an 8% inflation rate (and that's a fairly normal rate of medical cost inflation) and the original $100 cost is, twenty years later, more than $466. The $100 a day your parent will receive will only cover about a fifth of today's costs.

As such, be sure the policy comes with inflation protection. In particular, you want compounded inflation protection rather than simple inflation protection. With simple protection, the original policy amount increases by a set percentage each year. Sticking with that same $100 daily coverage, a simple 5% inflation adjustment means the addition of $5 in coverage every year. After twenty years, the policy pays $200 a day.

Compounded protection is much better. A $100 per day policy compounded at 5% a year will pay out $265 a day in twenty years.

The costs: This is the single most significant reason people do not buy long-term care insurance.

The American Association of Long-Term Care Insurance in its 2009 study of 155,000 individual policies found that the average buyer between ages forty-five and fifty-four paid $1,900 a year for a policy. The range stretched from $1,000 to $3,200.

Beyond age fifty-four, LTC policies are all over the map, based on age and policy coverage.

A sixty-year-old, for instance, might pay between $500 and $600 a year for minimal coverage, and $5,000 or more for so-called Cadillac coverage. At eighty, the same person might pay upward of $2,000 a year for the minimal plan, and in excess of $10,000 for the Cadillac plan, assuming the eighty-year-old would qualify for coverage to begin with or that an LTC underwriter would even sell the plan to an eighty-year-old.

(Very broadly speaking, a minimal policy might include daily benefits of $100, no inflation adjustment, and coverage that stops after two years or sooner, depending on how quickly the lifetime benefits are consumed. Cadillac coverage, meanwhile, might include daily benefits of $250, a 5% compounded inflation adjustment annually, and unlimited lifetime benefits.)

Here's a chart giving you a general feel for LTC premium costs at various age ranges:

The Cost of LTC Insurance		
Initial Purchase Age	Minimal Coverage	Cadillac Coverage
60	$500–$600	$5,000–$6,000
70	$1,000–$1,250	$8,500–$10,000
80	$1,500–$2,000+	$10,000+ assuming insurer will write coverage

One of the biggest concerns potential buyers of LTC policies have is the possibility that the insurance company will unexpectedly raise premiums. That is a risk, and it's a risk that harmed many consumers in the early days of LTC policies. Indeed, numerous media accounts exist of LTC buyers who ended up having to drop their coverage because the insurance company hiked rates so high that policyholders could no longer afford the insurance.

The fact is that unlike most types of insurance, LTC premiums are not locked in when you buy. Insurers have the legal right to increase their premiums under certain circumstances.

And it has happened in the past. Often these events are associated with lower-rated insurers who jump into the market with lowball pricing just to build a book of business quickly. Then, once policyholders start filing claims and the insurer realizes it doesn't have enough income coming in to cover the claims it's receiving, the insurer jacks up the premiums to either raise income or force policyholders (the insurer's cost center) to drop coverage.

States have put the kibosh on those tactics, so they're not

very common anymore. Nevertheless, you need to be aware of them so you can protect your parents.

One prime way to avoid this is to make sure your parents don't buy the cheapest LTC policy they can find. Policies that are priced well below comparable policies are a risk. That's often the sign of an insurer trying to quickly build business.

Instead, make certain that the insurer your parent chooses has an A. M. Best rating of A+ or A++ (the "superior" ratings). Even that is not a 100% guarantee that a chosen insurer won't raise rates. But insurers carrying such a rating are the strongest in the industry, and they usually become the strongest by employing sound practices, meaning they're generally not trolling for customers by slapping cheap prices on their policies, only to have to jack up rates later.

TIP: Pay attention to so-called nonforfeiture clauses. This clause states that if Mom/Dad must stop paying on an LTC policy for whatever reason, they do not give up all benefits. Instead, they will remain eligible for reduced benefits up to the amount of money they invested in the policy before dropping coverage.

Most states require insurers to offer a nonforfeiture clause. And some states require insurers to provide a "contingent nonforfeiture clause" when a policyholder drops coverage because the insurer raised premiums by a certain percentage. In practical terms this means that even if Mom/Dad did not originally choose to pay for a nonforfeiture benefit, they are entitled to it if the insurer raises premiums by a certain amount.

Cutting the Cost of LTC Premiums

As with any other form of insurance, savvy consumers can trim their long-term care costs by increasing the policy's deductible. Only with LTC policies, the deductible isn't called a "deductible." It's called the "elimination period." This is a term you need to know, because it is a key component to buying LTC insurance.

Unlike traditional deductibles that specify a dollar amount that the insured person must first pay before insurance kicks in, the elimination period specifies a number of days that the insured person must first cover before the LTC policy takes over.

Most insurers price their policies with a ninety-day elimination period, meaning Mom/Dad must pay for the first ninety days of costs associated with long-term care needs.

Increasing the number of days Mom/Dad covers those costs is, in practical terms, the same as raising the deductible.

Numerous independent insurance analysts (pros unaffiliated with any insurance company and who, instead, are paid to determine if an insurance policy is worth the cost) have come to the conclusion that LTC plans with high elimination periods are generally more valuable.

Here's why: Increasing the elimination period can substantially reduce the costs of the policy, sometimes by 50% or more, depending on the length of the elimination period. Remember I told you my wife and I bought LTC policies? Well, our elimination period is a *year*, and it reduced our costs dramatically from the ninety-day period the insurer originally quoted.

Your first thought, rightly, should be: But wait, that means Mom/Dad's out-of-pocket costs will increase, since they will have to pay for more days on their own until the policy kicks in.

That's true. However, reducing the costs makes the policy affordable, meaning Mom/Dad can buy coverage in the first place. It can also make a better caliber of coverage more affordable. Instead of affording daily benefits of $100 with a ninety-day elimination period, your parent might be able to afford $150 or even $200 a day with a six-month or one-year elimination period. Or maybe it means that instead of affording a policy providing just two years of coverage, your parent can afford coverage for five years, or maybe even lifetime benefits.

The real cost of long-term care isn't the first year; it's the outlying years, when Mom/Dad's ongoing LTC needs threaten to overrun the policy's coverage period. If a policy ends after two years, but your parent is still alive and in need of care for another three, five, or ten years, what then?

With LTC policies, you want Mom/Dad to buy as much bang as their bucks can afford, and in this case "bang" means as many years of coverage or as much daily benefit as possible, just to be on the safe side. Yes, that means potentially that your parent will never use all the coverage they've paid for. But that's the risk of getting old. Still, when you're talking about the enormous costs of long-term care year after year, and at a time when medical/pharmaceutical advancements mean people are increasingly living into their nineties and toward one hundred, it's better to have more coverage than you ulti-

mately need than to have less. Having less means Mom/
Dad—and ultimately you—have to worry about how to
pay for potentially years of care once the policy runs out.

As such, LTC is best used as a catastrophic insurance
plan. Don't view it as the immediate source of money to
pay for long-term care needs. View it as the source of
money that kicks in right when the costs of LTC threaten
to spiral out of control. Mom/Dad will pay more money
out of their pocket early on, but they'll be able to afford
greater coverage and, likely, preserve a chunk of their
assets.

As you go about managing your parent's health-related
issues, I encourage you to call on the experiences of friends
and colleagues who orbit your world. Many of them will have
navigated this world, or are navigating it currently. They
can be of enormous assistance in terms of helping you cope
with the stress that is commonplace, they can guide you to
the people and resources they've found most helpful and/or
useful, and they can show you the shortcuts they found to
help them more quickly or efficiently deal with any of the
headaches that will arise. I won't tell you this is easy. It's frustrating, infuriating, sad, mentally draining, and, sometimes,
thankless.

But there is a certain sense of accomplishment you will
feel in overcoming a health care system that can be as soul-
less as it is perplexing. And at the end of the day, you will
know you've made your parent's life a little easier because
you cared enough to fight the fight.

Conclusion

As I sit here writing these final pages in late summer 2010, I find myself a customer of my own book.

My maternal grandmother, who along with my grandfather raised me, has reached the point in her life where much of what you've just read now applies to her—and, alas, me. She is eighty-nine years old. She struggled with and beat cancer a few years ago, but the fight left her frail of body. Her mind now moves slower than it did for the woman who spent her fifties and sixties taking care of me. She lives on a fixed income, and I have in recent months helped her navigate a reverse mortgage so that she would have income to pay for some of her medical care, to eliminate the mortgage payment she still had, and to replace an ancient air-conditioning system. I have befriended her banker so that he can keep me in the loop with her finances, and so that he knows to call me when any issue arises in her accounts.

Now she is increasingly in need of medical assistance to manage doctors' appointments, keep tabs on what medications she's taking, and provide wound care for a nasty gash on her leg that she sustained while climbing out of the bathtub.

In all of this I'm lucky in two ways.

First, my grandmother *wanted* to have The Talk with me. While visiting her one day a few years ago, she told me she was collecting various papers, insurance documents, bank account information, and whatnot, and that she would be calling me in a few weeks to come over and talk about her financial life. She knew she was getting old and wanted someone she trusted to make sure she was doing the right things, and to make sure someone knew where all her important papers were when the time to deal with them arrived.

Second, I have my wife, who happens to be a registered nurse and who has spent her career working for HMOs, hospitals, and within the medical administrative ranks. She knows the world my grandmother interacts with regularly now, and she has assumed a great deal of the medical burden because she can more easily and, most important, more effectively navigate it than can I. This has been a tremendous help.

Nevertheless, I'm now being called into duty for a task that, honestly, I never wanted to think about. Though she carries the title "grandmother," she is in all practical terms my mom, given how much love, effort, and sacrifice she put into raising me. As such, I know from firsthand experience that going through all of these processes and strategies and— yes—chores for a loved one is mentally taxing and emotionally draining.

But it can—and it must—be done.

You can allow your parents to do it alone, and then pick up the pieces when they fall. You can allow a stranger to take control, never quite certain if that person is working in your parent's best interest, or is conflicted by self-interests. Or, you can take the reins and do it yourself, which is clearly the direction I'm pushing you with this book.

I think it's imperative that an elderly person's offspring take up the mantle of parent to your parents. Maybe I've traveled too much and interacted with too many cultures where age is revered, but aging parents, in most cases, have earned the right to rely on their children for assistance with the chores, duties, obligations, and necessities of aging.

And when you take on this duty, you step into a special role that comes with its own silent oath. You are agreeing to protect Mom and/or Dad, to stand up for their best interests, to fight the fights they no longer can. Sadly—and frustratingly—I wrote too many times in my seventeen-year career as a *Wall Street Journal* finance reporter about the scumbags who prey on seniors: the family members who rob parents/grandparents, the creepy hangers-on who feign friendship in order to lay claim surreptitiously to assets or to convince an elderly acquaintance to alter a will, the lowlife financial products peddlers hawking inappropriate investments to the elderly for the sole purpose of lining their own nest to the detriment of their aged clients.

Alas, the crimes continue, and you're there to protect Mom/Dad and their money from these predators of the elderly. You're also there to make sure their finances are in order, and to help secure the care necessary to live at home or in the institution of their choosing. You are an advisor and a confidant, and if you don't know the best solution to whatever issue Mom/Dad confronts, you're the gofer who hunts down the right person to provide it. You are the child who can return the love they have given you, to give them a sense of security in a scary time—a time when they don't have the answers (or even know the right questions). You are the person to help them when no one else can or will.

I'll close out this book with the singularly brilliant movie *Crash*. There is an underlying story line in that film in which Matt Dillon's character, a bitter Los Angeles cop, is adrift in the medical system as he seeks care for a father who struggles with intense pain from a swollen prostate. Except the medical system refuses to acknowledge the need for surgery because the cost-obsessed primary care doctor assigned to the case continues to define the problem as a low-level urinary tract infection. As the movie concludes, a poignant scene: A father and son are in the bathroom, Dad sitting on the toilet, clearly pained, unable to relieve his need. As the father breaks into tears, all the son can do is hug his father and kiss him on the head.

As that wrenching bathroom scene unfolds, a melancholy Bird York song, "In the Deep," plays: "Life keeps tumbling your heart in circles till you . . . let go."

It is an all-too-appropriate image with all-too-appropriate lyrics that perfectly capture what you face when your parents, like your children, become your responsibility.

But I say that not to be depressing or to make you question why you would want such a painful duty in the first place.

To the contrary. I want that scene to offer . . . inspiration, really. You can be lost in the system like the L.A. cop, or you can choose to take control so that you don't helplessly watch your parents struggle inside the system, whatever system it might be.

Yes, caring for the needs of your aging parents will be challenging. It will be heartbreaking. Frustrating. Mind-numbing. At times you will want to cry. You will want to scream. You will want to reach through the phone line and strangle the financial advisor or insurance company representative or health care worker who continues to give you the runaround when you simply want the answer to a very basic yet important question related to your parent's needs.

And that's OK. You are not alone.

With this book, you now have the tools you need. You know where to find the information necessary to help Mom/Dad navigate the hurdles of old age. You know the questions to ask, the traps to avoid and the tips that can help you better manage your parent's affairs.

Basically what I'm saying is that *you can do this*.

And you will find in doing so that your parents—and you—will be better off because of the love, the time, and the effort you put into helping them live more happily and securely in the final years of life.

Terms to Know

adjusted gross income (or AGI): The income upon which a taxpayer owes annual taxes. This is your total income from all sources, minus specific deductions.

annuity: An insurance-related financial contract that guarantees a specific amount of income to the contract holder, either over a predetermined number of years or for the contract holder's remaining lifetime.

arbitration: A dispute resolution process that takes place outside a court of law and in which an impartial third party hears the facts of a case and determines the outcome in a legally binding decision.

back-end fees: These are common with mutual funds and are typically associated with "B-shares." These fees are a contingent deferred sales charge, in which a mutual fund company charges additional annual fees to fundholders in order to cover the cost of the commission that the fund originally paid to the broker or agent who sold the fund to a client. The fees continue for as long as the investor owns the shares.

benchmark: The standard by which an investment is measured so that investors can compare the returns they receive in a mutual fund vs. what they could have received in a similar investment. In general, a mutual fund that owns a broad basket of U.S. blue-chip stocks benchmarks its performance against the Standard & Poor's 500 stock index. Beating the index regularly—or at least coming close to matching it—is good. Routinely underperforming the benchmark is bad.

beneficiary: The person or persons who are designated to receive property in the event the property's owner dies.

blue-chip stocks: Large, high-quality companies that trade in the stock market. These are typically well-known companies that have a long, demonstrated history of growth and that often, though not always, pay a dividend.

bonds (see also government bonds, corporate bonds, and municipal bonds): A financial instrument through which governments and companies issue debt to raise money. The bond itself is the borrower's promise to repay the debt with interest over a predetermined period of time. Interest payments are usually made semiannually. Some bonds generate income that is tax-free, like those issued by cities and states; some generate income that benefits from reduced tax exposure, such as U.S. government Treasury bonds; and the income from some, particularly corporate bonds, is fully taxed. At maturity, the borrower repays the principal, though in some cases issuers have defaulted. Still, bonds are largely considered safer than stocks, which do not guarantee that the original principal will be repaid.

certificate of deposit (or CD): An investment contract issued mainly by banks, credit unions, and brokerage firms. CDs pay a predetermined amount of interest, and the contract specifies the amount of time the money must remain on deposit, usually one month to five years. CDs are insured by the Federal Deposit Insurance Corporation (FDIC) for up to the current $250,000 limit per customer, per account.

Consumer Price Index (or CPI): The U.S. government–produced indicator of inflation. The Bureau of Labor Statistics publishes the CPI monthly. Though the agency produces multiple versions, the CPI-U, covering America's urban prices, is the most widely reported figure. The media routinely pull out what they term "the volatile food and energy components" in the CPI to provide the so-called core inflation number. The reality, of course, is that consumers cannot conveniently pull the volatile food and energy prices from their monthly costs.

conservatorship (same as guardianship): The legal right given to you or another person to manage the property and financial assets of a parent who is incapable of providing prudent management.

corporate bonds (see also bonds): Debt issued by companies. Corporate bonds generally mature in one to thirty years, though some companies—such as Walt Disney—have famously issued one-hundred-year bonds, or "century bonds." Income from corporate bonds typically is taxed as "ordinary income," meaning at the same rates at which paychecks are taxed; those are often the highest rates.

cost basis: The original cost of an asset. If your parent paid $5 a share to buy shares of Walmart, that's the cost basis. In real estate terms, it's the original cost of the property, plus the improvements made during the years.

currencies: Monetary units such as the U.S. dollar, the Japanese yen, and others that countries use to facilitate commerce. In investing terms, currencies are an asset that some people own to diversify a portfolio away from exposure to the dollar.

currency trading account: An investment account in which the account holder can trade currencies. These are typically leveraged accounts, meaning each dollar invested is multiple, often four to five hundred times the original level, allowing an investor to control a larger sum of money with a relatively small grubstake.

direct deposit: An electronic transfer payment in which distributions such as a paycheck, a Social Security check, or an income tax return are deposited into a checking account automatically. No physical checks are sent. The payer sends the payment electronically between two financial institutions. Direct deposit is a safer, more efficient means of receiving payment because it eliminates the possibility that a physical check is lost, stolen, or misplaced.

dividend: A share of the profits that a company pays to its shareholders on a regular basis. Companies typically pay dividends every quarter, though some pay annually.

eldercare: The term given to the process of providing care to the elderly. "Care" in this instance can mean everything from helping with physical and mental health care needs to financial and estate planning.

estate planning: Arranging legal and financial affairs so that your wishes regarding the distribution of assets and property to heirs are executed after your death.

exchange-traded fund (or ETF): An investment that acts like a mutual fund but is traded on an exchange like a share of stock. ETFs own a basket of stocks, and their price changes continually throughout the day, based on the value of the underlying shares. Unlike mutual funds that investors can buy and sell once a day after the market closes, ETFs are open to trading throughout the day, providing far greater flexibility. They are designed to shadow an index of some sort, like the Standard & Poor's 500, or any of scores of other indexes in the United States and abroad.

Federal Reserve: The governmental agency that serves as America's central bank. The Fed, as it's widely called, sets monetary policy for the United States by regulating the flow of money and credit in the economy. The Federal Reserve's Federal Open Market Committee, or FOMC, gathers generally monthly to set interest rates.

fiduciary or fiduciary duty: A person or a legal entity assigned the task of administering assets or financial affairs for another person. A fiduciary duty legally binds a fiduciary to act in the best interest of the person for whom assets are being managed.

401(k) plan: A retirement savings plan offered by companies. Employees contribute money from their paycheck to their plan, while, in many instances—though not all—a company will kick in a small contribution as well. The money a worker contributes is tax deferred, meaning the cash isn't taxed until it is withdrawn in retirement. The benefit is that the deferral reduces tax obligations during the accumulation phase. Typically, 401(k) plans offer a limited variety of preselected mutual funds for workers to choose from, though some plans offer access to individual stocks as well. Investors are eligible to begin withdrawing money when they are fifty-nine and a half; prior to that the IRS imposes a penalty equal to 10% of the money withdrawn. Regardless of when money is withdrawn, an investor will owe taxes equal to the investor's ordinary income tax rate in the year the cash comes out of the account.

guardianship (see conservatorship)

government bonds (see also corporate bonds and municipal bonds): Also known as Treasury bonds. These are debt obligations of the U.S. government, and because the government guarantees the payment of accumulated interest and the repayment of principal they are considered the world's safest investment.

home equity line of credit (or HELOC, pronounced "he-lock"): A line of credit at a bank, savings and loan, or credit union that allows homeowners to tap into the equity in their house. Most have floating interest rates, meaning that as the Federal Reserve raises and lowers interest rates, the interest rate on HELOCs changes.

home equity loan: Effectively the same as a HELOC, though the interest rate is often fixed.

ID theft (or identity theft): Fraudulently assuming the identity of another person, often to commit financial crimes using credit cards in that person's name or by illegally accessing that person's financial accounts.

immediate annuity: An investment contract issued by an insurance company through which an investor trades a lump sum of cash for a guaranteed stream of typically monthly payments that begin immediately. The payments can last a preset number of years or for an investor's remaining lifetime. Once an immediate annuity begins to pay out, the investor cannot cancel the contract or reclaim the original principal.

index funds (see also mutual fund, exchange-traded fund): A mutual fund or an ETF that is designed to track a specific index, such as the Standard & Poor's 500. Index funds can track stock or bond indexes, real estate, or commodities like gold and agriculture.

individual retirement account (or IRA): A tax deferred retirement savings account. Depending on the taxpayer's annual income level, annual contributions to an IRA can be used to reduce your taxable income each year. The money in the account grows tax deferred, meaning interest, dividend, and capital gains that accumulate inside the IRA are not taxed until the investor begins withdrawing the money. Investors are eligible to begin withdrawing money from an IRA at age fifty-nine and a half; prior to that they are subject to an early withdrawal penalty equal to 10% of the sum withdrawn. No matter when the money comes out, income taxes are imposed on the sum withdrawn, and the rate is equal to the investor's so-called ordinary income tax rate in a given year.

know your customer: The rule by which banks and other financial institutions must do appropriate due diligence on a customer to ascertain relevant financial information. In the context of this book, "know your customer" means that a bank, brokerage firm, or insurance company needs to know what products are and, more important, are not suitable for the client.

laddering: The concept of splitting your money across multiple certificates of deposit, or CDs. Each CD matures at a different time, so that you might have, for example, five CDs with one maturing each year for five years. CD one matures after one year, CD two after two years, etc. The purpose is to generate the greatest amount of income while maintaining decent liquidity.

long-term care (or LTC): An insurance contract that promises to cover the costs of aging that are not generally covered by private insurance or Medicare/Medicaid. These include the costs of a nursing home, assisted living center, adult day care, in-home care provider, and the like.

maturity date: One of the key data points for bonds and certificates of deposit. This is the date upon which the original principal is returned to the investor.

Medicaid: A federal- and state-funded system designed to provide health care to the needy. In most cases, recipients must be essentially impoverished before applying for coverage.

Medicare: A federally administered program providing health insurance to those age sixty-five or older.

money market (money market account, money market mutual fund): Technically a market in which short-term debt instruments—often of thirty days or less—are bought and sold. Money market accounts and money market funds are investments in which the returns are derived from investments that trade in the money market.

municipal bond (or muni bonds; see also bonds, corporate bonds, and government bonds): Debt issues by cities, states, and local municipalities to fund everything from daily government operations to schools, hospitals, parks, and other such expenses. Interest paid on muni bonds is typically—though not always—free of all local, state, and federal taxes.

mutual funds (see also index funds, exchange-traded funds): An investment in which investors own a fund that holds shares of multiple companies. A mutual fund provides an investor instant and far greater diversification than would be possible with a given sum of money.

ordinary income rates: The tax rates the IRS applies to income including that received from salaries, interest, and dividends, among other sources. Ordinary rates tend to be the highest rates in the tax code.

permanent life insurance: A form of insurance such as whole life or universal life that is designed to be held permanently by the insured person. Permanent life insurance typically combines life insurance with a savings component. This is often the most expensive form of life insurance.

power of attorney: A legal document that authorizes you or someone else to act on behalf of another person, such as your parent.

principal: The original amount an investor places in an investment.

reverse mortgage: A mortgage available only to homeowners age sixty-two and older. A reverse mortgage allows a senior to access a portion of a home's equity and provides a lump-sum payout, a line of credit, or an ongoing stream of income.

required minimum distribution: The amount of money a person must withdraw from a traditional IRA each year after reaching age seventy and a half. Failure to comply results in penalties paid to the Internal Revenue Service.

return of investment (or return of capital): A payment in which all or a portion of the income is the original principal put into the investment.

return on investment: A measure, in percentage terms, of the gain or loss generated on the original principal.

Roth IRA (see also individual retirement account): Similar to an individual retirement account except that Roth IRAs grow tax-free, meaning you owe no taxes on the interest, dividends, and capital gains each year, nor do you owe taxes when you withdraw the funds. That's because unlike a traditional IRA you get no tax benefit when investing in a Roth IRA, meaning you cannot deduct the annual contribution on your tax return each year.

second mortgage: A loan on a piece of property that is secured by that property. The loan, however, is subordinate to a first mortgage, the original existing mortgage on that property.

Standard & Poor's 500 stock index (or S&P 500): A much-watched index of five hundred stocks, representing the largest publicly traded companies in America. It is the benchmark by which investors gauge the performance of most mutual funds.

stocks: Partial ownership of a publicly traded company. This is also known as "equity." Stocks convey ownership of a share of the income stream a company generates and any dividends it distributes. Stockholders are also eligible to vote on company matters when they come up each year.

suitability: A requirement that agents for financial and/or insurance firms offer customers investments that fit an investor's needs based on factors including age, financial background, income, and risk tolerance.

tax deferred: An investment in which the taxes that are due each year are deferred until after the age fifty-nine and a half. Tax deferral is common with variable annuities, 401(k) plans, and most IRAs.

term life insurance: A form of life insurance in which the coverage remains in place for a specified number of years. These are basic policies that provide a preset amount of coverage, known as the death benefit. Unlike permanent life insurance, they do not include a savings component. Term life is often the most cost-effective insurance.

trailing commission: A recurring revenue stream that sellers of insurance, annuities, and mutual funds often earn for selling a particular financial product. So long as the investor owns the product, the agent continues to receive commissions for some period of time. These types of commissions typically incentivize the agent at the expense of the customer.

transfer agent: The financial agency, often a bank, hired to keep records of who buys and sells a particular company's stock and bonds. The transfer agent is also responsible for distributing dividends.

Uniform Lifetime Table: A life expectancy table based on actuarial data. These are primarily used by insurance and annuity firms to determine how long a potential policyholder is likely to live and, thus, how to price the policy.

variable annuity: An insurance contract that promises to pay at a later date a stream of income that can last a preset number of years or until death. The annuity combines an insurance contract with mutual fund–like subaccounts that rise or fall based on the value of investments inside those subaccounts. Because variable annuities are generally used to accumulate assets prior to retirement, they're often ill suited for those already in retirement.

wealth management: Financial planning, mainly for wealthy individuals, that incorporates asset/investment management with estate and tax planning services and, when needed, legal resources.

will: The legal declaration by which a person, at death, transfers his/her property to heirs.

The Talk Worksheet, Part 1

Personal Data			
Full name:			
Birth date:			
Social Security #:			
Maiden name:			
Current address:			
Previous addresses:			

		Pension?	
Former employers / employment dates:		Yes	No
		Yes	No
		Yes	No
Employee ID #s (for pensions and/or insurance benefits):			

Financial Account Data			

	Bank branch	Box #	Key location	Home-safe combination
Safe deposit box:				_____

	Firm name	Account/ policy type	Account number	Contact info	Notes/ policy coverage online login/ passwords
Bank	____ ____ ____ ____	____ ____ ____ ____	____ ____ ____ ____	____ ____ ____ ____	____ ____ ____ ____
Invest. accts.	____ ____ ____	____ ____ ____	____ ____ ____	____ ____ ____	____ ____ ____
Insurance policies	____ ____ ____ ____	____ ____ ____ ____	____ ____ ____ ____	____ ____ ____ ____	____ ____ ____ ____
Employer pensions	____ ____ ____ ____	____ ____ ____ ____	____ ____ ____ ____	____ ____ ____ ____	____ ____ ____ ____
IRA / 401(k)	____ ____ ____ ____	____ ____ ____ ____	____ ____ ____ ____	____ ____ ____ ____	____ ____ ____ ____
Misc. accts. / credit cards	____ ____ ____ ____	____ ____ ____ ____	____ ____ ____ ____	____ ____ ____ ____	____ ____ ____ ____

The Talk Worksheet, Part 2

Documents for which you need to keep copies	
Document	**Location**
Wills	
Trusts	
Living wills	
Durable power of attorney	
Durable power of attorney/health care	
Insurance policies (declations page)	
HIPAA authorization	
Revocable living trust	

Utility providers		
Utility	**Account #**	**Contact information**
Electricity		
Gas/heating oil		
Water		
Telephone		
Cable TV		
Internet		
Security company		
Revocable living trust		

Index

Note: Page numbers followed by a *t* refer to text boxes or tables.

BOOKS BY JEFF D. OPDYKE

PROTECTING YOUR PARENTS' MONEY
The Essential Guide to Helping Mom and Dad Navigate the Finances of Retirement

ISBN 978-0-06-135820-3 (paperback)

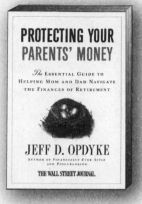

Jeff D. Opdyke offers a comprehensive guide to address one of the most poignant—and often confusing and difficult—transitions in life: becoming a parent to your parents. Aside from addressing various financial matters, Opdyke helps bridge the communication barrier between parents and adult children that can make the transition more difficult than it needs to be.

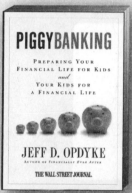

PIGGYBANKING
Preparing Your Financial Life for Kids and Your Kids for a Financial Life

ISBN 978-0-06-135819-7 (paperback)

When couples are planning their financial lives together, few questions are as significant as how to afford a family. To help couples meet this challenge, personal finance writer Jeff D. Opdyke lays out everything they need to do to prepare for the expense of having kids, and how to handle the obligation of teaching their kids about money.

FINANCIALLY EVER AFTER
The Couples' Guide to Managing Money

ISBN 978-0-06-135818-0 (paperback)

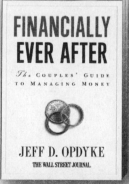

Too often with money, couples face two choices: fight and risk making the situation worse, or keep quiet and risk making the situation worse. *Financially Ever After* offers a third option: family financial fluency— the insight, knowledge, and vocabulary every couple needs to communicate effectively about money.